George Washington's War

IN CARICATURE AND PRINT

George Washington's War

IN CARICATURE AND PRINT

KENNETH BAKER

GRUB STREET | LONDON

For my grandchildren – Tess, Conrad, Oonagh, Evie, Fraser and Stanley

Published by
Grub Street Publishing
4 Rainham Close
London
SW11 6SS

British Library Cataloguing in Publication Data

Baker, Kenneth, 1934-
George Washington's war in caricature and print.
1. United States--History--Revolution, 1775-1783-- Caricatures and cartoons.
2. English wit and humour, Pictorial.
I. Title
973.3'0222-dc22

ISBN-13: 9781906502539

Designed by Lizzie B Design
Maps by Eugene Fleury

Grub Street Publishing uses only FSC (Forest Stewardship Council) paper for its books

Contents

Introduction

'A most accursed, wicked, barbarous, cruel, unnatural, unjust and diabolical war.' Chatham

AMERICANS REVERE THEIR REVOLUTIONARY WAR OF INDEPENDENCE from 1776–1783. The foundation of this great nation, like the formative years of other nations, is peopled with heroes – some grand, some eloquent, some humble and homespun, many incredibly brave and all pitting their courage and determination against the most powerful country in the world, led by a despot, ruled by an effete aristocracy and served by a brutal army. The British view of this unmitigated disaster is that Americans were very lucky since they could not have won alone and only the intervention of France – Britain's oldest enemy – allowed a colonial rebellion to succeed.

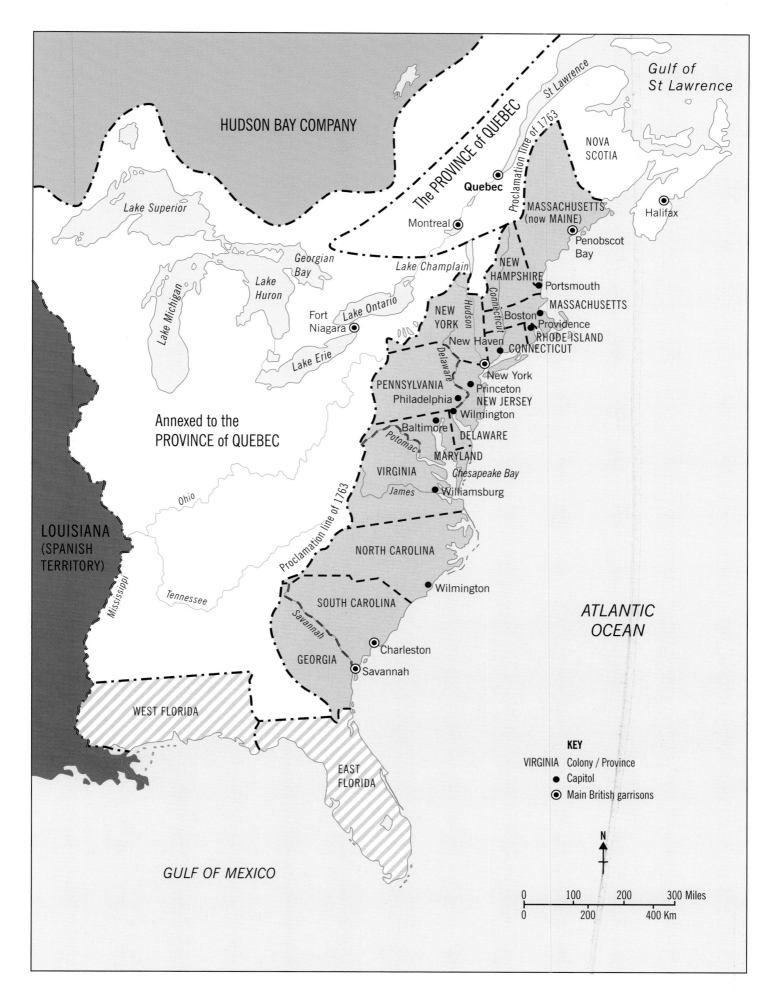

HUDSON BAY COMPANY

Gulf of St Lawrence

The PROVINCE of QUEBEC

St Lawrence

Proclamation line of 1763

NOVA SCOTIA

⊙ **Quebec**

MASSACHUSETTS (now MAINE)

⊙ Halifax

Lake Superior

Montreal ⊙

Penobscot Bay

Georgian Bay

Lake Champlain

NEW HAMPSHIRE

● Portsmouth

Lake Huron

Lake Michigan

Fort Niagara ⊙

Lake Ontario

Lake Erie

NEW YORK

Hudson

Connecticut

● Boston

MASSACHUSETTS

Providence ●

New Haven ●

RHODE ISLAND

CONNECTICUT

⊙ New York

PENNSYLVANIA

● Princeton

NEW JERSEY

Philadelphia ●

Annexed to the PROVINCE of QUEBEC

● Wilmington

Delaware

DELAWARE

Baltimore ●

Potomac

MARYLAND

LOUISIANA (SPANISH TERRITORY)

Ohio

VIRGINIA

Chesapeake Bay

James

● Williamsburg

Proclamation line of 1763

Mississippi

Tennessee

NORTH CAROLINA

● Wilmington

SOUTH CAROLINA

Savannah

ATLANTIC OCEAN

GEORGIA

⊙ Charleston

⊙ Savannah

WEST FLORIDA

EAST FLORIDA

GULF OF MEXICO

KEY

VIRGINIA Colony / Province

● Capitol

⊙ Main British garrisons

N

0   100   200   300 Miles

0   200   400 Km

By coming afresh to this war, which I had last read about at school, I was able to disentangle the myths of both sides for the rather less glamorous truth. Most of the pictures of the war that Americans hold dear to their hearts were painted in the 19th century to depict the heroic foundation story. It was a challenge to go back to the contemporary prints and caricatures to see how they reflected what was happening when it happened, for caricatures are like snapshots capturing a moment in the shutter of the artist's eye.

In the 1770s, London had a flourishing print trade and many of these prints are in this book; most are overwhelmingly in favour of America. In contrast, the art of engraving had barely reached America; the most experienced engraver was Paul Revere, who was also a publisher and a silversmith, and the handful of his caricatures were based on British originals with some of the characters transposed. The other difficulty was that when people are fighting to the death for their freedom and independence, satire is not seen as a weapon of war and there are virtually no graphic attacks by Americans on the British. By quarrying the fine collections of libraries and historical societies on the East Coast of America, however I have been able to find some quite rare and unfamiliar caricatures and contemporary prints, some of which have not been published before.

Between 1773-1782, America came to dominate British politics. The government led by Lord North was thrown onto the defensive by the brilliant oratory of the leaders of the Whigs, Chatham, Charles James Fox and Burke. In London there were many supporters of America, quite apart from the merchants and manufacturers who saw their export market closed through the war, but the defence of the government was left to the Prime Minister (the First Lord of the Treasury), Lord North who, by his own admission, was totally inadequate as a war leader.

Lord North and King George III bear a heavy responsibility for Britain's humiliating defeat. North decided to levy the dormant duty on tea that had been introduced earlier by Townshend and it was this that ignited the spark of revolution in Boston by asserting the sovereignty of the Westminster Parliament to tax its colonies. The revolutionary agitators in Boston were opposing the powers of Parliament not the powers of George III, but as the King so vehemently supported his government they were glad to direct their fire on him. By his strong personal commitment – 'the colonies must either submit or triumph' – George became the bogeyman for the Americans; many of whom still regard him as a wicked despot. Whenever Lord North faltered, which he did on many occasions, George insisted that the war had to continue until Britain won.

It was the first time in the history of Britain that a king and his government had to deal with the problems of holding together an empire overseas. The colonies in India, the West Indies, and North America were all considered to be subject to the Crown. But the American colonists were so different from the Maharajahs and Princes of India, and the plantation owners of the West Indies. They carried with them many of the instincts of the constitutional pioneers who had created the parliamentary system in England; they had a spirit of independence and enquiry; the suspicion of an over-powerful monarch; and a devotion to free speech and the rule of law. The only political arrangement that may have suited them would have been some concept of a commonwealth: a free and self-governing association happy to recognise allegiance to one monarch as all their traditions originated from the country over which their monarch reigned. But such a compromise, a possibility in 1763, had by 1775 become impossible through folly, ignorance and stubbornness. There were powerful forces at work which would have crushed a greater man than George III.

From the start, America had many advantages. The first was the sheer size of the American wilderness – forests, mountains, large lakes, fast-flowing rivers, cliffs, gullies, swamps and marshes, and there were few roads and even fewer bridges. An army of 50,000 which was the size of the British and German force in 1781 could not hold down such a vast country.

Secondly, there was the sheer problem of running a war from London that was taking place some 3,000 miles away. The instructions of the War Secretary, Germain, and the Navy Secretary, Sandwich, took two or three months to reach the men on the ground. In 1775-76, of the 40 transport ships that set out from Britain for the port of Boston, only eight arrived safely there: some were blown to other ports and some seized by privateers. As Burke said, 'Seas roll and months pass between order and execution.'

Thirdly, there was the question of leadership. Britain needed a great general – a Marlborough, or a Wellington, or a Wolfe, or a Montgomery – but instead they had a bunch of second-raters – Howe, Clinton, Burgoyne, and Cornwallis. Some were good field-commanders, but they lacked the energy and spirit to follow-up and pursue the enemy ruthlessly. Each wanted to deliver the 'knock-out' blow to Washington and as each pursued his personal campaign, jealously and envy mingled with vainglory. Howe could have crushed Washington in 1776; Howe and Clinton failed to cooperate to save Burgoyne: Clinton, as Commander-in-Chief, resented Cornwallis' popularity with his men and for his part Cornwallis could barely conceal his contempt for his senior officer.

America in its moment of need found, not a great general, but a great leader. Washington was a poor commander in the field – losing more battles than were won, but he created and sustained the American Continental Army, ensuring that in six years of fighting it was not annihilated. That meant he had to avoid the 'knock-out' battle which resulted in many inglorious retreats, but he held his army together and without that the revolution would have collapsed.

The AMERICAN COLONIES.

Britain had superior fighting force and with better leadership it could have crushed the American army. But that alone would not have given victory: the war had become a civil war – America's first – between those loyal to King George and those who wanted independence. Like all civil wars, there was excessive savagery: neighbours killed neighbours; and there were revenge executions and land-grabs. The war had started with the aim to crush a rebellion but after five years Cornwallis recognised the shift to bolstering and protecting the loyalists:

'The great object of his Majesty's force in this country is to protect and secure his Majesty's faithful and loyal subjects and to encourage and assist them in arming and opposing the tyranny and oppression of the rebels.'

This was too great a task. British forces could hold a few garrisons – New York, Charleston, Savannah – but even when they won battles in the surrounding countryside the rebels would fade away, only to reappear as soon as the redcoats had left to seize the land and the slaves of the loyalists and if necessary kill them. The forces of King George could not guarantee the safety of his loyal subjects.

It was not just, however, a colonial rebellion or a civil war: it became a world war. Britain's foreign policy after the great victory of 1763 was focussed on expanding its overseas territories through its naval superiority. It neglected Europe and the powers in Europe, thirsting to revenge their humiliation,

The American Colonies

This engraving by George Bickham, one of the leading London engravers, appeared in 1743 in a book describing the American colonies. Little was known about this vast continent and its British settlers since for the merchants of London, Bristol and Liverpool the West Indies were significantly more important. This is an idealised conception: an Indian brave clearly at peace with the elegant Englishman who is being offered two pipes by a Negro slave, emphasising that tobacco was the most important export to Europe. So little was known, so little appreciated, so little anticipated.

seized the opportunity. Within three years of Lexington, France entered the war, a year later Spain, and then Holland. Britain had to fight on many fronts. The French and Spanish fleets, when combined, were more than a match for the British navy.

Washington by himself could never have won a decisive victory. The best he could hope for through his delaying tactics was to sap Britain's staying power. What gave him victory in 1781 was the intervention of the French fleet which led to the ultimate humiliation of Cornwallis' surrender at Yorktown in 1781. It is indeed ironic that the ancient regime of France gave victory to the revolutionary republican America, but by so doing added to the enormous financial burden that was to lead to its own revolution. Britain had started the war and France had ended it: both were victims of the law of unintended consequences.

Chapter One

The Path to Revolution 1763-1773

'Let no man be dismayed at being proclaimed a Rebel'
Virginia Gazette

THE SEVEN YEARS WAR, 1756-1763, was a triumph for Britain and the Treaty of Paris that concluded it in 1763 greatly extended the British Empire. France lost Canada and all her lands east of the Mississippi; all its stations in India but four; and some of its West Indian islands. Spain had to yield Florida to the British but gained Louisiana from France. It seemed a triumph that France, Britain's old enemy, had been thrust out of North America but it had an unexpected and unintended consequence. The thirteen colonies had needed British soldiers to protect them from the French but now that threat had disappeared – a disappearance reinforced by the supremacy in the Atlantic and the Caribbean of the British navy which had 800 ships and 70,000 sailors – a new relationship between the mother country and its colonies was about to unfold. With this new security the colonies would be able to develop their interests in their own way; expand westwards; trade more freely; trust to their own militias; and gain the confidence to run their own governments. The spirit of independence arose from the triumph of British arms.

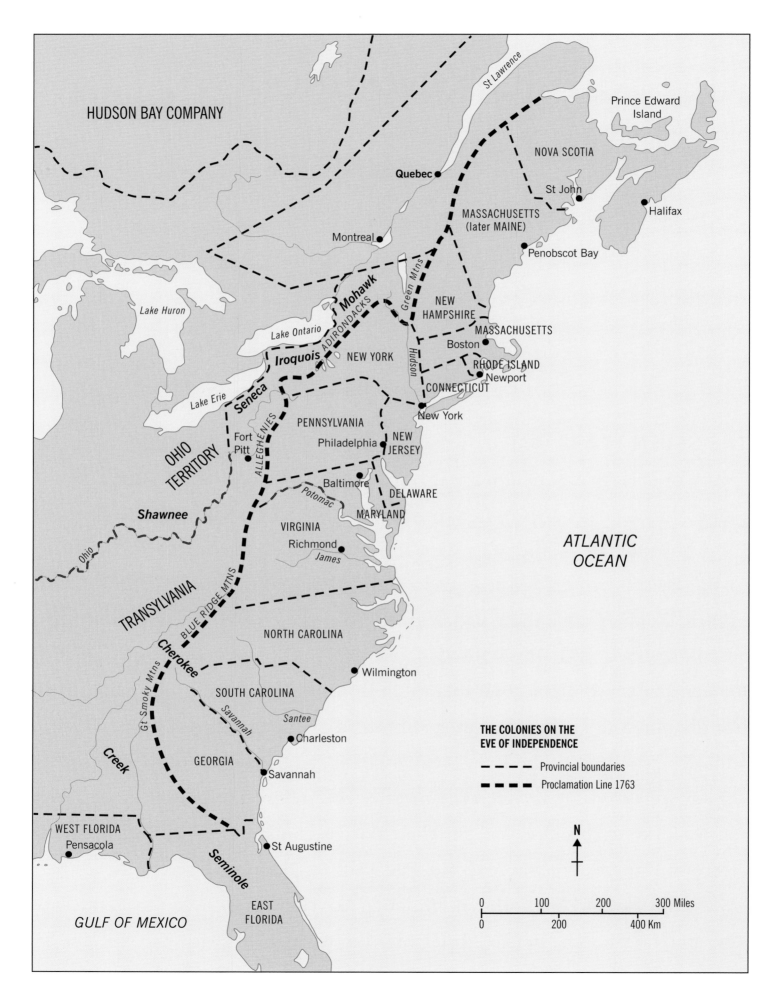

HUDSON BAY COMPANY

St Lawrence

Prince Edward
Island

NOVA SCOTIA

Quebec

St John

Halifax

MASSACHUSETTS
(later MAINE)

Montreal

Penobscot Bay

Mohawk

Lake Huron

Green Mtns

NEW
HAMPSHIRE

Lake Ontario

ADIRONDACKS

MASSACHUSETTS

Boston

Iroquois

NEW YORK

RHODE ISLAND
Newport

Hudson

Seneca

Lake Erie

CONNECTICUT

ALLEGHENIES

PENNSYLVANIA

New York

OHIO
TERRITORY

Fort
Pitt

Philadelphia

NEW
JERSEY

Shawnee

Baltimore

DELAWARE

Potomac

MARYLAND

Ohio

VIRGINIA

Richmond

ATLANTIC
OCEAN

James

TRANSYLVANIA

BLUE RIDGE MTNS

NORTH CAROLINA

Gt Smoky Mtns

Cherokee

Wilmington

SOUTH CAROLINA

Savannah

Santee

Creek

GEORGIA

Charleston

THE COLONIES ON THE
EVE OF INDEPENDENCE

– – – Provincial boundaries

▬ ▬ Proclamation Line 1763

Savannah

WEST FLORIDA
Pensacola

Seminole

St Augustine

N

0   100   200   300 Miles

0   200   400 Km

GULF OF MEXICO

EAST
FLORIDA

In this success were planted the seeds that were to lead to an independent America. Before the war the thirteen American colonies were largely self-governing – they raised their own taxes, organised their own trade, had their own courts and were allowed to get on with their own lives. Above all the Yankees wanted to be left alone to get on with their own affairs in their own way. Ten years later the first American Continental Congress was to meet and pass resolutions yearning for the 'good old days' before 1763.

After the war the London government was forced to realise that it had a large empire in North America – some three million people compared to Britain's seven million. The British army that had protected the colonists in the wars were also needed to protect them from Native American Indians, and to police the thinly populated areas of Canada and Florida, and further marauding attacks from France could not be ruled out. Not unreasonably the Prime Minister, George Grenville, thought that American citizens should contribute towards their own defence – hence the Sugar Act 1764 and the Stamp Act 1765.

The Sugar Act imposed a duty on sugar and had two purposes. The first was to protect the sugar industry of the West Indies by banning supplies from Spanish and French territories, reflecting the influence of Jamaican sugar barons in the House of Commons. It disrupted the flourishing trade of smuggling which was the foundation of the fortunes of many American merchants who had no spokesmen in London. The second purpose was for the revenue from the duty to defray the costs of defending the colonies by maintaining a British army of 10,000 men. This was not un-reasonable for Britain's debt in 1763 at the end of the war was £60 million higher than in 1756, the beginning.

Benjamin Franklin in April 1764 pointed out that the British were acting against their own self-interest: 'For Interest with you we have but little: the West Indies vastly outweigh us of the Northern Colonies. What we get above Subsistence we lay out for you with your Manufactures. Therefore what you get from us in Taxes, you must lose in Trade. The Cat can yield but its Skin.'

In 1765 Grenville decided to extend the principle of the colonies contributing towards the cost of maintaining an army by introducing a Stamp Act levied on all manner of documents. It seemed sensible as stamp taxes were levied in Britain and in the West Indies. In America it was a disaster as it hit the most articulate people: lawyers, printers, publishers, journalists, academics, merchants, newspaper editors and readers. It threatened the very existence of a free press which went into overdrive, by placing a skulls-head on their mastheads. Colonial troops could not protect the officials appointed to collect the tax and not one penny was collected. Boston merchants boycotted British goods which led to British merchants in Glasgow, Bristol, Liverpool and London telling a commons committee that businesses were being badly hit and the act had to be repealed. That was the clinching argument for Grenville's successor, Rockingham, when in 1766 he repealed it. It is not surprising that this surrender was greeted in Boston with 'Ringing of all the Bells in Town, Guns Firing, Drums Beating and all Sorts of Musik'.

AMERICA STAMPED
26 Dec. 1764

The Proclamation Line (opposite)

It suits Americans to portray the Revolution as a band of brave and intrepid freedom fighters standing up against arbitrary taxation and military occupation. There were also other forces at work. In 1763 the British government, to protect the traditional land of the Indian tribes, laid down a line from north to south to prevent any of the thirteen colonies acquiring land to the west of it. This was bitterly resented as the colonies wanted to expand into the agriculturally rich areas beyond the mountains where many of the revolutionary leaders, including Franklin and Washington, had made speculative purchases. It was even worse after the Quebec Act of 1774 which extended the territory of Quebec to the Mississippi including the Ohio Valley. In effect, Canada had moved hundreds of miles south. The Americans resented the action of a distant government in curbing their own imperialism and to them this was infinitely more important than a few pence on a pound of tea. George Washington described the line as 'a temporary expedient to quiet the minds of the Indians and (which) must fall of course in a few years.'

America Stamped
26 December 1764

The Boston Gazette
7 October 1765
This graphically relates the hated Stamp Act to both death and piracy.

The Pennsylvania Journal (below)
31 October 1765
The day before the Stamp Act came into force, William Bradford, the editor of *The Pennsylvania Journal* (which his grandfather had founded in 1742) openly asked whether 'any Methods could be found to elude the Chains forged for us and escape insupportable Slavery, which it is hoped, from the last Representation, now made against that Act may be affected?' So even as early as this the rhetoric was inflammatory – 'chains' and 'slavery'. Bradford was also willing to play his own part as a leading 'Son of Liberty' and helped to pay for a drum to summon a Stamp Act mob. In 1777 he suspended the Journal as he had joined the militias to resist the British advances at Trenton and Princeton.

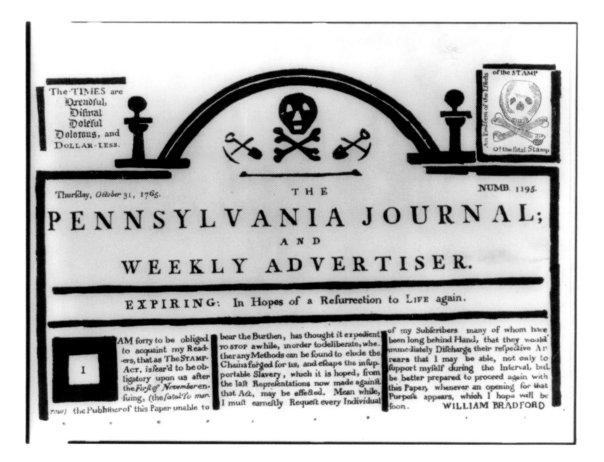

View of the Year 1765
27 January 1766
Paul Revere

The Stamp Act is a dragon supported by two devils which are trying to snatch Magna Carta from a man holding a drawn sword labelled 'B' which represents Boston. He is supported by Rhode Island, New York, Virginia, the Dutch Provinces, and Hampden who had protested against Charles I's ship money. Pym, another hero of the English Civil War, lies dead. On the right John Huske, who had gone to England from New Hampshire, been elected to the House of Commons and become a prominent supporter of the Stamp Act, is hanged in effigy on the Liberty Tree. The actual hanging took place on 1 November and not the date shown on the tree.

This is the first satirical print by Paul Revere. He was an engraver, not an artist, who produced all manner of items: trade cards, clock advertisements, bookplates, portraits, and Masonic certificates. He was not a creative satirist, but was very effective in turning his hand to propaganda. This print is an almost exact and very good copy of an English print of 1763 showing British politicians attacking the Excise Tax of that year which had nothing to do with America. There is no content similarity between the two and the Liberty Tree is an original addition.

The Repeal, or The Funeral of Miss Ame-Stamp
18 March 1766

In 1765 George Grenville the Prime Minister (1763-1765), with the enthusiastic support of George III, had introduced the Stamp Tax similar to that in Britain. On the day that it was due to come into force, 1 November 1765, there was a riot in New York as it was seen as unconstitutional and unfair. In February 1766 the new Prime Minister, Rockingham, decided to repeal the act and George III was cheered in the streets.

In this print bales of stamps have been returned from America; a statue honouring Pitt is to be shipped there as he had condemned the tax eloquently; one of the ships is named Rockingham; Grenville reluctantly carries the coffin; Bute is the chief mourner in plaid breeches; and the warehouses of the manufacturing towns are open for business again.

The print was so popular that within four days 2,000 copies were sold and pirated copies from the fifth impression sold in their thousands.

. An . Attempt to land a Bishop in America.

An Attempt to land a Bishop in America
1768
The Political Register

Every branch of Christianity was well represented in the colonies: the Congregationalists in Massachusetts and Connecticut; Quakers in Pennsylvania; Anglicans in the Carolinas and Virginia; the Dutch Church in New York; and Catholics in Maryland. After the end of the war with France, the Archbishop of Canterbury, Seeker, was keen to send a bishop to consolidate the Anglican position but his discreet lobbying got to the ears of dissenters in Boston who exploded angrily against 'a flood of episcopacy'. The government for a change got it right. After the failure of the Stamp Act and the furore over the Townsend tax, they did not want to pour oil onto the flames. This apocryphal print foresees that any bishop would be forced to flee. The crowd shout for liberty of conscience and ominously 'No Lords Spiritual or Temporal in New England'. John Adams' view was that the ordinary people would find British bishops just as unacceptable as British taxes. From 1765 an evangelical movement known as the 'Great Awakening' swept through the colonies. This condemned sinfulness, luxury and corruption all of which were the gifts of England. Their biblically supported vision of a new future inspired and reinforced the secular revolutionary spirit and the challenge to authority implicit in that. In 1771 the loyalist Anglican clergy in New York and New Jersey in a petition for a new bishop warned 'independency in Religion will naturally produce republicanism in the state'.

Britain could not yield with grace. As the most powerful and successful country in Europe, it was used to winning, asserting, and laying down terms. Confident and proud that it had the best system of government in the world, it did not need to argue, concur or concede. This led to the House of Commons passing without a division the Declaratory Act which asserted that Parliament could pass laws affecting the American colonies on virtually anything. This fig-leaf was to turn into a poisonous thorn of provocation in the body politic of America.

Although the settlers welcomed the British suppression of the rising of Pontiac, the Ottawa Chief who in 1763 had seized most of the western outposts apart from Detroit and had killed over 200 settlers, they did not want the London government to act as a protector of the Native American Indians. But this was what Grenville decided to do. In order to prevent a series of Native American Indian uprisings, he acted to protect their

ancient hunting grounds by issuing a proclamation in 1763 which in effect set a limit on the expansion of all thirteen colonies. Governors were not allowed to grant land west of a line drawn vertically down the country west of the Appalachian Mountains and Mississippi. Many of the colonists, including George Washington, had acquired land speculatively in just those areas and resented London's interference in their own brand of imperialism.

In June 1767 Charles Townshend, the Chancellor of the Exchequer in Pitt's administration, introduced further duties on goods imported into America – glass, lead, paper, printers' colours and tea. He tightened controls on smuggling and set up a Board of Customs Commissioners in Boston to administer the act. It was the Stamp Act writ large because virtually all paper came from Britain, so once again the liberty of the press was at risk. Within weeks a movement to boycott British goods swept

A Warm Place in Hell
8 July 1768
Paul Revere

This is Revere's second satirical print and it refers to the stand taken by the Massachusetts House of Representatives in February when they approved a motion condemning all the acts that levied taxes on the colonies and sent it to all the other state legislatures. London ordered the Governor, Bernard, to instruct the legislature to rescind its vote and if it did not, he would disband the General Court. However in another vote in June the House reaffirmed its position with 92 members voting in favour and 17 against. The 92 became the toast of Boston and Revere was also commissioned to make a large silver punchbowl bearing the names of the leading patriots.

The print shows the devil driving the 17 into the jaws of Hell led by an active loyalist, Timothy Ruggles. This print is a copy, and in fact a much improved copy, of an English print of 1765 in which Bute, Fox and other English politicians are being pushed into Hell. This shows that English prints did find their way to America and that was how George III and English politicians, like North and Wilkes, were recognisable figures.

through the colonies and New England's trade with Britain was cut by half in 1769. After three years the duties were an embarrassment as their yield barely exceeded the cost of collection and so in 1770 they were removed. But fatally the tax on tea was retained, by the margin of just one vote in the Cabinet, to show that the government in London still had the right to tax the colonies. By that time Townshend was dead: Horace Walpole penned this valediction: 'He had almost every great talent...if he had had but common truth, common sincerity, common honesty, common modesty, common steadiness, common courage, and commonsense.'

After the repeal of the Townshend duties there were few issues that kept the revolutionary flames burning brightly. When Benjamin Franklin released some old letters from Hutchinson, the Governor of Massachusetts, which he had come across, advocating tougher measures against rebellious colonists, the Massachusetts legislature passed a motion demanding the dismissal of the governor, but it was not a big enough issue for the other colonies to take up. This frustrated Sam Adams, the principal political agitator in Massachusetts, from 1765-1775, but it was difficult even for him to make bricks without straw.

Adams engendered and then kept alive the spirit of opposition to colonial rule, principally through the press by turning small slights into major injustices and by organising gatherings in various states of 'concerned citizens' – self-elected representatives – which created a growing sense of togetherness for he got them to correspond with each other. He also worked busily to glorify the 'Sons of Liberty' and to harass government officials – he was the master of 'rent-a-mob'. Based in Boston he turned the killing of five Americans in a local riot in 1770 into an unprovoked

The Colonies Reduced (below)
August 1768
The Political Register

This prophetic print depicts Britannia being lopped of her limbs – her colonies. Virginia and New England had led the campaign against the Stamp Act and Grenville's attempt to enforce the billeting of soldiers on private homes in Virginia in 1765 had to be abandoned. *The Political Register*, a sharp critic of the government's American policy, is here publishing an image first used by Benjamin Franklin in 1766 when he was in London putting America's case. He printed it on cards that were handed to MPs before debates.

massacre which had to be celebrated annually forever after. But by far his most effective weapon was the use of the press where he would provoke controversy usually by writing letters under pseudonyms both for and against an issue. Sam Adams should be recognised as the first American to master the art of propaganda: the patron of spin said that 'to put your enemy in the wrong and keep him so is a wise maxim in politics as well as in war'.

In 1773 there were 31 local newspapers from New Hampshire to Georgia and being over-whelmingly Whig they were hostile to the colonial government. For the previous ten years they had fostered a growing resentment at the increasing intrusiveness of the government in London. The most patriotic – or virulent in the eyes of the colonial government – were *The Boston Gazette* and *Massachusetts Spy*, but they were closely followed by *The Pennsylvania Gazette*, owned by Benjamin Franklin, *The New York Gazette*, *Weekly Postboy*, *The Virginia Gazette*, and *The New Hampshire Gazette*. The effect of these papers was so great that when Gage proclaimed martial law in June 1774, he lashed out at the press and the pamphlets for 'the grossest forgeries, calumnies and absurdities that ever insulted human understanding'. The Tories had lost the propaganda war. It is indeed ironic that one of the great and enduring freedoms of Britain – the freedom of the press – became a powerful weapon directed at the very heart of British rule.

In 1763 the spirit of revolution was barely sputtering, but by 1773 it was burning brightly. Just as today the internet carries details of how to make bombs, Nathaniel Ame's Almanack of 1775, supplied practical directions for making gunpowder. The government in London had little idea of how much the revolutionary fervour had built up in the years from 1763-1775.

Lord God Omnipotent (opposite)
3 November 1768
Paul Revere

This, Paul Revere's third satire, was commissioned as a frontispiece for *The Northern Almanack* for 1769 by the Boston publishing house, Edes and Gills. It shows Britain as an imperial queen and America as a forlorn figure in 'the utmost Agonies of Distress and Horror'. The wrecked ships seem to represent the wrecked hopes of America and it reminds the good people of Boston that on 28 September, a British fleet had arrived in Boston and regiments of redcoats had landed on 1 October. In this print God does not seem to be doing much about it.

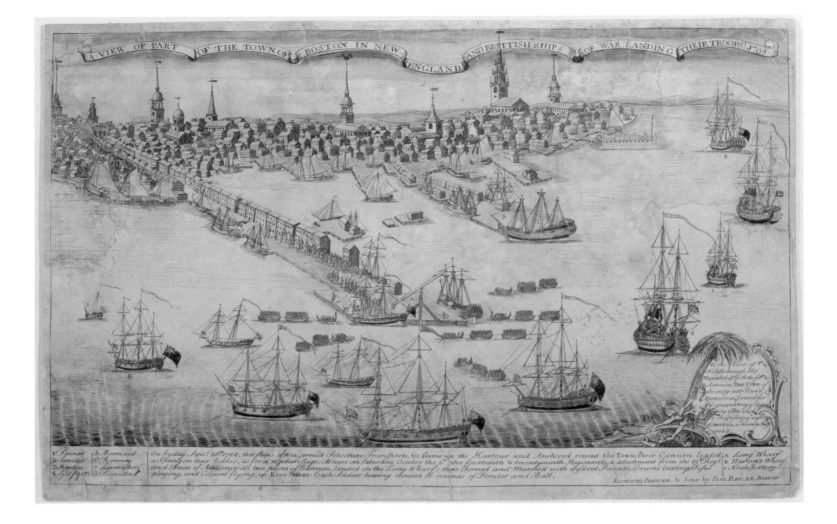

A VIEW OF PART OF THE TOWN OF BOSTON IN NEW ENGLAND AND BRITTISH SHIPS OF WAR LANDING THEIR TROOPS! 1768

Landing of the Troops
30 September 1768
Drawn in 1770 by Christian Remick, engraved by Paul Revere

This was published two years after the event, but the inscription is blatantly patriotic:

'The fourteenth and twenty-ninth Regiments...landed on the Long Wharf; there Formed and Marched with insolent Parade, Drums beating, Pipes playing, and Colours flying up King Street.'

The Sons of Liberty in Boston wrote to John Wilkes, who was in prison in London, and he replied: 'I have read with grief and indignation the proceeding of the ministry with regard to the troops ordered to Boston, as if it were the capital of a province belonging to our enemies, or in the possession of rebels. Asiatic despotism does not present a picture more odious...' Wilkes gave the Sons of Liberty permission to quote his letter but prudently they decided against.

John Hancock

Hancock's inherited wealth was increased through smuggling. Following the Townshend duties Hancock headed the committee which rallied merchants to organise a boycott of goods imported from Britain. In 1769 the pro-British newspaper, *The Boston Chronicle*, printed the names of merchants who were cheating and bringing in goods, including Hancock whom they dubbed 'Johnny Dupe'. Even *The Newport Mercury* which supported the rebels reported that Hancock was 'getting rich by receiving freight on goods made contraband by the colonies'. The house belonging to Mein, the editor of *The Boston Chronicle* was attacked – windows broken, walls covered with filth – and when he was tracked down by a mob he fled to a ship before seeking safety in England. Hancock's vanity was exploited by Sam Adams and for a short time he seemed to be the leader of the rebel cause, becoming the first President of the Continental Congress, but he was bitterly disappointed when Washington was appointed Commander-in-Chief. Having served his purpose as the leading merchant against Britain's trade restrictions, Hancock was quietly relegated to a more minor role – John Adams' comment was, 'Such a leaky vessel is this worthy Gentleman'.

N.º V Engraved for Roy.ˡ American Magazine Vol.I

MAGNA CHARTA

P. Revere ſc

The Hon.ᵇˡᵉ JOHN HANCOCK. Eſq.ʳ

Political Electricity
1770

This is a cameo from a larger print which shows London in the background described as Boston, and the busy workers of Boston vigorously pursuing their various trades – felling a tree, shearing cloth, making a shoe, grinding coffee or corn. The title boasts that 'The Coasts of America where ye Inhabitants are Industrious in every Act to provide themselves with ye Manufacturers that Great Britain used to furnish them with, being constrained & drove as it were to Industry, by ye late Ministerial harsh Proceedings, in forcing ye Stamp and other Acts of Internal Taxes upon them contrary to ye true Spirit of British Policy, & which sooner or later this Kingdom will rue ye Imprudence of The City of London transferr'd to Boston.' London can sink into corruption and tyranny but Boston will flourish through its own enterprise and energy.

Laſt Thurſday, agreeable to a general Requeſt of the Inhabitants, and by the Conſent of Parents and Friends, were carried to their *Grave* in Succeſſion, the Bodies of *Samuel Gray, Samuel Maverick, James Caldwell,* and *Criſpus Attucks,* the unhappy Victims who fell in the bloody Maſſacre of the Monday Evening preceeding!

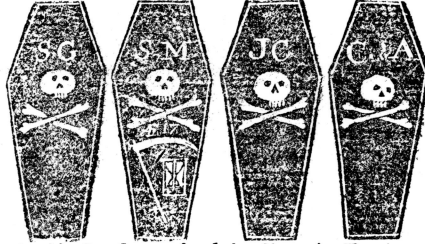

On this Occaſion moſt of the Shops in Town were ſhut, all the Bells were ordered to toll a ſolemn Peal, as were alſo thoſe in the neighboring Towns of Charleſtown Roxbury, &c.

The Boston Gazette
12 March 1770
Paul Revere

The four coffins represent Samuel Grey, Samuel Maverick, James Caldwell and Crispus Attucks. *The Boston Gazette* could not resist this dramatic piece of anti-British propaganda and were glad to report that the four victims were given what amounted to a state funeral.

The Bloody Massacre perpetrated in King Street, Boston
1770
Paul Revere

On 5 March a hostile, jeering mob taunted a British sentry outside the Customs House in Boston. To protect him seven soldiers and an officer emerged from the guardhouse and within a few minutes five Americans were shot dead. This is a blatant piece of American propaganda as the dead man is depicted as white but he was in fact black. A further marksman is shown firing from a window, which simply did not happen. The redcoats did not line up and open fire, they were attacked by men with clubs, and in the subsequent trial six were acquitted of manslaughter. Their defence lawyer, John Adams, a cousin of the leading anti-royalist, Samuel Adams, and later the second President of the United States, argued that they had been assaulted by a 'motley rabble of saucy boys, negroes and mulatoes, Irish teagues and jack tarres'.

This print was 'designed' by Paul Revere, an engraver and silversmith, who was to become famous for his ride in 1775 to bring the news that the British army was moving to attack Concord. However, he had stolen the idea from Henry Pelham who accused him of doing 'one of the most dishonourable Actions you could be guilty of'. This print appeared in Boston, but it was copied and sold in England where it bore the title, 'The Friends of Arbitrary Power – or – the Bloody Massacre'.

M.ʳ SAMUEL ADAMS.

Mr Samuel Adams

Paul Revere

This engraving is based on Copley's portrait of Sam Adams. It was commissioned by the *Royal American Magazine* which had a short life from January 1774 to March 1775. Paul Revere was its principal engraver, providing them with thirteen engravings.

Sam Adams, a firebrand at Harvard and bitter about his failure in business, turned himself into a brilliant success as an agitator against British colonial rule – today he would be called an urban terrorist: an idealist who was fanatical and unscrupulous. Based in Boston he wrote articles and letters under pseudonyms for sympathetic newspapers like the *Massachusetts Chronicle*. He was a revolutionary organiser who could whip up a mob, organise a gang, turn a slight into a vicious insult, intrigue, plot and coin inflammatory phrases. He dubbed the Boston newspapers, 'those scourges of Tyranny'. He was implacable and ruthless in his hatred of the British.

On the day of the Boston Tea Party in the densely packed meeting in the Old South Church, it was he who gave the signal for action by declaring, 'This meeting can do nothing more to save the country'. The crowd poured out of the church and headed for Griffins Wharf. Gage's spies had identified him as the major ringleader – little wonder the British wanted to arrest him in Concord.

The British Government did not listen keenly enough to the clear advice from their servants in America: Gage who had demanded more troops, or Sir James Wright's plaintive question from Georgia to Dartmouth, 'No Troops, no Money, no orders or Instructions, and a wild Multitude gathering fast, what can any Man do in such a situation?'

By then America was clearly divided between the loyalists, the Tories, who looked to London and to George III as the guiding authorities for the colonies, and the rebels, the Whigs, who wanted to be more in control of their own affairs, although many of them professed loyalty to the King over the water. The very freedoms they cherished and wanted to entrench in their own country were learnt from English history – they were impressed by the words of Hampden, Pym and Locke. But the redcoats of the army whose protection in the Seven Years War they had needed and welcomed, had become the 'lobster-backs' of an alien force that did not understand their way of life.

The politicians in London, not one of whom had visited America, failed to appreciate that their Empire in the thirteen colonies was fundamentally different and infinitely more advanced than their other possessions in the West Indies and India. There was more than an aura of sophistication; in the towns there were fine houses, paved streets, meeting halls, churches built from classic English designs, shipping, insurance and fire companies, a mass of newspapers, schools, colleges, a university, circulating libraries, representative assemblies, a flourishing ship-building industry, and in the north an extensive iron-forging industry financed by local capital and producing more than in Britain. They also had their own courts, militias and prisons. But there was no large aristocratic class and so their leaders were merchants, lawyers, planters and farmers. Apart from slavery it was a more egalitarian society as Carleton, the Governor General of Canada, hit upon in 1768: 'The British Form of government transplanted into this Continent never will produce the same Fruits as at Home. A popular Assembly which preserves its full Vigor, and in a Country where all Men appear nearly upon a Level, must give a strong Bias to Republican Principles.'

Ten long years of mistakes and misunderstandings had created a spirit of revolution. John Adams reflected in his later life, 'The Revolution was affected before the war commenced. The Revolution was in the minds and hearts of the people.'

Chapter Two

Friends and Enemies

'The blood of the slain, the weeping voice of nature cries, "T'is time to part".'
Tom Paine

THE FRIENDS AND ENEMIES OF AMERICA in Britain from 1763 not only reflected their own personal views but they also mirrored the parties or groups to which they belonged. The Rockingham Whigs, whether in office or opposition, generally favoured America, but Rockingham was no radical – he sensibly repealed the Stamp Act but foolishly passed the Declaratory Act. His disciple, Edmund Burke, was more consistent. In April 1774 in his famous speech on American taxation he was amazed that the politicians for ten years had allowed a situation that, 'So paltry a sum as three pence in the eyes of a financier, so insignificant an article as tea in the eyes of a philosopher, have shaken the pillars of a commercial empire that ordered the whole globe.' In March 1775 he made his equally famous speech on Conciliations – 'I do not know the method of drawing up an indictment against a whole people.' The Chatham Whigs, with the clever young Shelburne, also favoured America and took their lead from their revered but ill leader. The young rising Whig, Charles James Fox, quickly decided to abandon North and take his chance in opposition – 'The noble Lord said that we are in the dilemma of conquering or abandoning America: if we are reduced to that I am for abandoning America.' Britain's most respected and senior general, Lord Jeffrey Amherst, refused to lead the armies in America, and Admiral Lord Augustus Keppel, Britain's most distinguished naval commander, also declined to serve.

Humbly dedicated to the Jacobine Clubs of France & England!!! by Common Sense
"These are your Gods, O, Israel!"

Pub May 28th 1791 by H. Humphrey
Nᵒ 8, 62 Bond Street

"Fathom & a half! Fathom & a half! Poor Tom!"

THE RIGHTS OF MAN; — or — TOMMY PAINE, the little American Taylor, taking the Measure of the CROWN, for a new Pair of Revolution-Breeches.

Thomas Paine
James Gillray

There is no print of Paine while he was in America. This one appeared in 1791 when he had sought refuge in France after he had written *Rights of Man*. His target was still the Crown and George III.

The Female Combatants or Who Shall
(opposite)
26 January 1776

Britain was already being depicted as the head of an Empire family. Here Britannia as the mother figure is having trouble with her rebellious daughter. As in many families, it's a struggle between Obedience and Liberty. Thomas Paine declared that the phrase, 'Mother Country', has been "Jesuitically adopted by the King and his parasites'.

They were ranged essentially against the King's ministers and the King himself. Grenville, the Prime Minister from 1763-1765, was personally totally convinced that Westminster had the right to levy taxes on America, a view strongly supported by his predecessor, Lord Bute. Grenville's successor, Rockingham, 1765-1766, repealed the Stamp Act but was only in office for less than a year.

His successor, Chatham, 1766-1768, although sympathetic to America did little to further its cause. Chatham's successor, Grafton, 1768-1770, was vaguely sympathetic to America but very weak and it was only after his resignation that he became more committed and supportive. His successor, Lord North, was totally committed to the policy that George III wanted.

The prints in London in the period of 1763-1783 were overwhelmingly in favour of America and anti-the British government and reinforced those urging peace. This creates an imbalance in the pictorial and visual history of the Revolutionary War which is not redressed by the handful of prints that were published in America. These were predictably patriotic since the rebels were fighting to throw off colonial rule and emerge as victors – there was no place for scepticism or satire. The loyalists did not think it necessary to commission any prints in favour of their cause for one very good reason: there were no trained engravers or etchers in America apart from Paul Revere, who was a committed patriot and moreover was not a creative satirical artist.

In London the friends of America easily won the arguments in the press and print media. They also had three of the most eloquent politicians – Chatham, Burke and Fox – but what they did not have were the numbers in the House of Commons. North was always able to put together a majority and this was reinforced by his two election victories of 1774 and 1780 – in the 18th century incumbent governments usually won. Until 1782 George III, therefore, could always count on a majority in both the Commons and the Lords – he won there while his armies were losing in America.

COMMON SENSE;

ADDRESSED TO THE

INHABITANTS

OF

A M E R I C A,

On the following interesting

S U B J E C T S.

I. Of the Origin and Design of Government in general, with concise Remarks on the English Constitution.

II. Of Monarchy and Hereditary Succession.

III. Thoughts on the present State of American Affairs.

IV. Of the present Ability of America, with some miscellaneous Reflections.

Man knows no Master save creating HEAVEN,
Or those whom choice and common good ordain.
                                    THOMSON.

PHILADELPHIA;

Printed, and Sold, by R. BELL, in Third-Street,

MDCCLXXVI.

Common Sense
10 January 1776
Thomas Paine

America's first bestseller – 100,000 copies were quickly sold. In his eyes Britain and its King were totally in the wrong and Americans rejoiced that an Englishman could write: 'the authority of Great Britain over this continent is a form of government which sooner or later must have an end....Everything that is right or reasonable pleads for separation, "TIS TIME TO PART.' This copy owned by the Boston Athenaeum bears George Washington's signature.

George was constant in his unflinching support of his governments. The Royal Proclamation in August 1775 stated bluntly that his American subjects were 'engaged in open and avowed rebellion'. The generals often complained of his ministers' inconsistencies, their ever-changing policies, and no follow-up, but the one rock that never moved was George III. It was not surprising therefore that he drew upon himself the hatred and ignominy of the American patriots. Sam Adams said, 'I have heard that George III is his own minister. Why, then, should we cast the odium upon his minions?' That is why the Declaration of Independence made him the evil centre of British tyranny charging him with eighteen offences including:

> *He has dissolved representative houses repeatedly....*
> *He has refused for a long time after such dissolutions to*
> *   cause others to be elected....*
> *He has made judges dependent on his will alone...*
> *He has kept among us, in times of peace, standing armies*
> *   without the consent of our legislatures....*
> *He has plundered our seas, ravaged our coasts,*
> *   burnt our towns....*
> *He is at this time transporting large armies of foreign*
> *   mercenaries to compleat the works of death, desolation*
> *   and tyranny.*

Sam Adams called this list George's 'catalogue of crimes'. He personalised the attack for the rebels needed a demon king and if necessary they would have invented one. Generations of Americans have learnt about George III from the Declaration of Independence. The personal charges are absurd since the decision to crush the rebellion and all that flowed from that was the policy of his ministers, strongly supported by the House of Commons. The Declaration of Independence is an astounding combination: a statement of lofty and memorable concepts penned by Jefferson; a blatant piece of propaganda; and, a farrago of nonsense about the personal power of George III.

Another friend who actually visited America was the writer, Tom Paine. The son of a poor Thetford corset-maker, he had tried his hand at many low paid jobs in London where he became appalled at the squalor, the drunkenness, the brutality of the poor and their ravaged, ragged lives. In October 1774, burning with a sense of social injustice, he left for America for a new start in a new land. Franklin, whom he had approached for help, thought he would make a teacher or a surveyor, but within a few months of arriving he was writing for the *Pennsylvania Magazine* in Philadelphia and rapidly became its editor. No lover of England, he quickly became a convert to independence and on 10 January 1776 he published a fifty-page pamphlet entitled, *Common Sense*.

Within weeks it became America's first bestseller. He found the words that the ordinary folk of America – the farmers,

The merchants, the lawyers, the soldiers and the delegates to the Continental Congress – wanted to hear. George III was 'the Royal Brute of Great Britain' and the British aristocracy exploited the lower classes of America: independence was the answer. He prophesised, 'T'is not the concern of a day, a year or an age; posterity are virtually involved in the contest, and will be more or less affected even to the end of time by the proceedings now.'

Paine recruited the English language to fight against English sovereignty. He was the first to coin the phrase 'The United States of America': his reward was later to be denied American citizenship. George Washington, encamped at Cambridge in the siege of Boston, recognised that Paine's pamphlet was 'working a powerful change there in the minds of men'. His own copy, inscribed on the title page in his own hand, is displayed today at the Boston Athenaeum. The rebel leaders embraced Paine's vision but John Adams was shrewd enough to recognise that *Common Sense* was too 'democratical'.

The Triumph of America
August 1766

Chatham is driving America on a coach towards a precipice where Britannia already lies – the horses are his ministers. Chatham was sympathetic to the colonies having opposed the Stamp Act and this print supposes the new government which he leads will bring in pro-American policies. Not a bit of it. He virtually neglected America, rejecting the idea of a separate Secretary of State for America, and even worse he allowed his Chancellor of the Exchequer, Townshend, to introduce further taxes directly aimed at the colonies. Apart from his gout, Chatham was subject to extended bouts of depression and at times he was literally out of his mind – one print hinted at his lunacy. He left the government in 1768 and until his death in 1778 he occasionally intervened, criticising North and pleading for a more sympathetic understanding of the American cause.

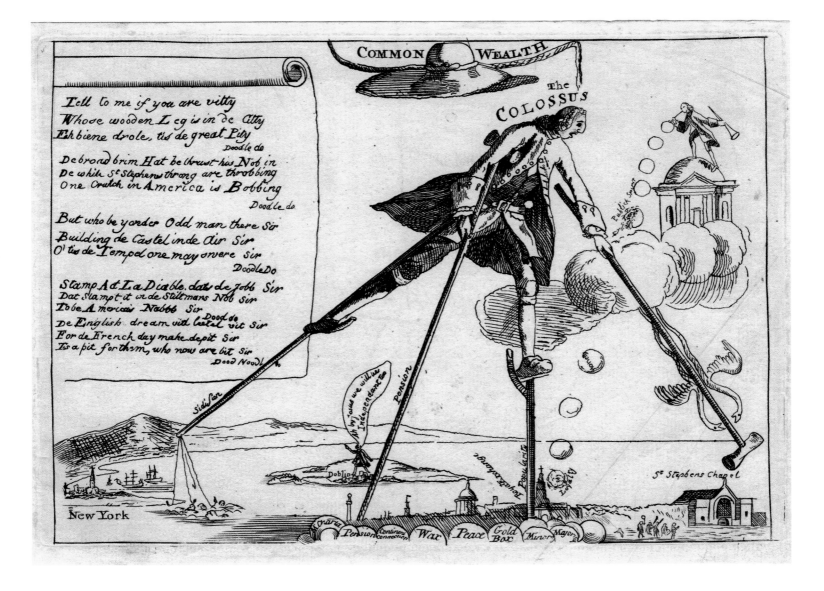

COMMON WEALTH

The COLOSSUS

Tell to me if you are vitty
Whose wooden Leg is in de City
Eh biene drole, tis de great Pity
                    Doodle de

De broad brim Hat be thrust his Nob in
De while St Stephens throng are throbbing
One Crutch in America is Bobbing
                    Doodle do

But who be yonder Odd man there Sir
Building de Castel in de Air Sir
O' tis de Temple one may onvere Sir
                    DoodleDo

Stamp Act La Diable. dat de Jobb Sir
Dat Stampt it in de Stilt mans Nob Sir
To be America's Nobb Sir
De English dream vid leetal vit Sir
For de French day make depit Sir
Tis a pit for them, who now are bit Sir
                    Dood Nood

New York

The Colossus
1766

In 1766 George lost his trust in his Prime Minister, Rockingham, and turned to his old bête-noir, the Elder Pitt. His government got off to a bad start for Pitt decided to leave the Commons, which he had dominated, to go to the Lords as the Earl of Chatham.

This unfavourable print shows one of Pitt's crutches supported by the City where he was always popular as trade followed the flag. Another crutch labelled 'Sedition' points to New York and is supporting some sinking rebels. Pitt was so popular that there were moves to erect statues of him in the colonies.

The Council of the Rulers & the Elders against the Tribe of ye Americanites (right)

1 January 1775

Westminster Magazine

This represents a meeting in the House of Commons where North commanded a majority secured through the distribution of places, pensions and favours. Here he passes a bag of gold to a supporter who is on the list of the King's friends. On his right, John Wilkes is trying to present his 'Remonstrance' against the government's policy which is futile for the King when opening Parliament in March 1774 had declared, 'You may depend upon my firm and steadfast resolution to withstand every attempt to weaken or impair the supreme authority of this legislature over the dominions of my Crown.' He said repeatedly that his government had to be supported as it was upholding the rights of Parliament, not the rights of the sovereign.

America In Flames

1 January 1775

Town and Country Magazine

Many people were alarmed at the repressive measures North had introduced. Mansfield blows on the flames of the bellows with the Massachusetts Bill, Bute with the Quebec Bill, while North peers through his lorgnette with the Boston Port Bill sticking out of his pocket, and a pot of tea rolls down the steps. The four trying to put out the fire includes Wilkes and are dubbed in the text of the magazine 'Patriots'. One cannot say that North was not warned.

The Political Cartoon, for the Year 1775.

America in Distress (opposite)

March 1775

Paul Revere, *Royal American Magazine*

This again is a copy of an English print, "Britannia in Distress", which appeared in 1770. The personalities and their comments are all changed: the politicians afflicting America, who has lost her Indian headdress and dropped her bow, quiver and arrows, are North, Mansfield, Bute and possibly Wedderburn. Those supporting America are Chatham on the extreme right, and Rockingham could be the figure who is fighting-off the government. Behind him is Sir William Beckford, the sympathetic Lord Mayor of London, who prophetically says, 'They will ruin her Constitution'.

The Political Cartoon of the Year 1775

1 May 1775

Westminster Magazine

George is being driven by Lord Mansfield in a carriage drawn by Pride and Obstinacy, and riding over Magna Carta and the constitution, into the abyss of the conflict with America which is in flames over the sea. Chatham, on his crutches, vainly waves as he foresees the disaster which is about to overwhelm his country. Some bishops and Lord North obsequiously watch the spectacle, and Lord Sandwich, celebrated for his lechery is paying a madame for her young prostitute. No one in England seems to care or appreciate that the devil is flying away with 'National Credit'.

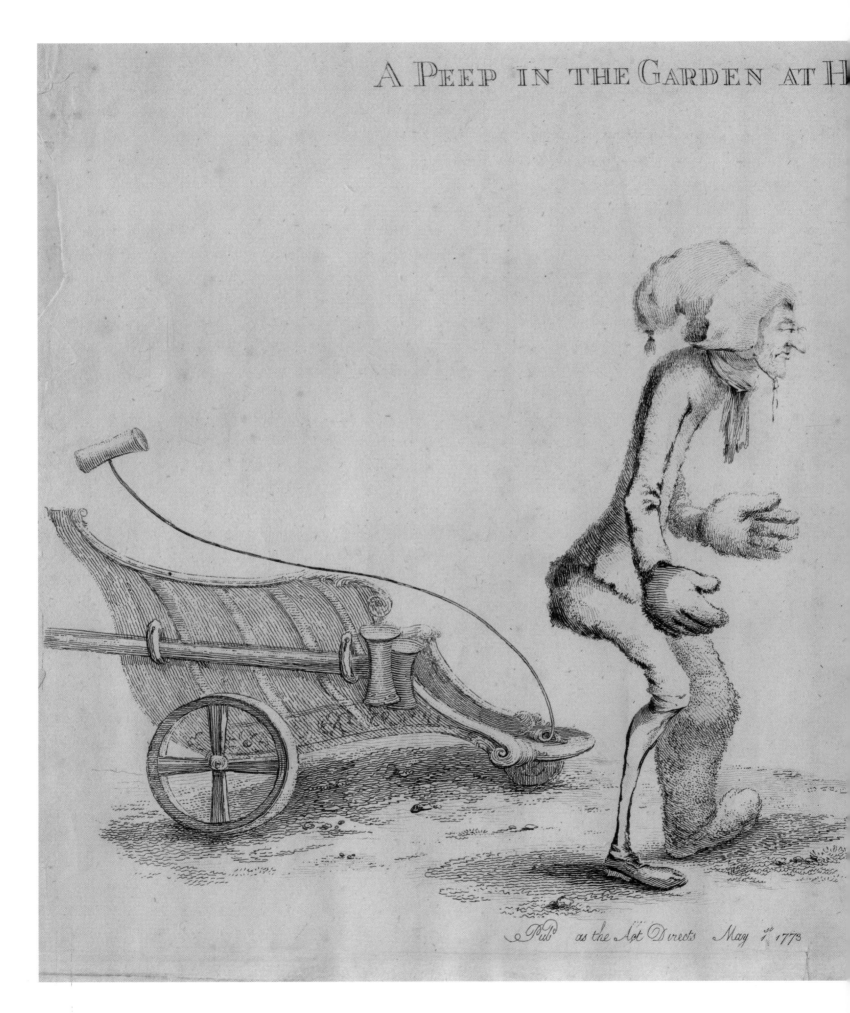

Pub.d as the Act Directs May 1.st 1773

A Peep in the Garden at Hayes
1 May 1773
W Austin

In this prescient scene the young Charles James Fox visits the old statesman, Chatham, who is raddled with gout: there is a distinct sense that the mantle is passing. Fox had entered the House of Commons in 1768 at the age of 19 and at this time was a minister in Lord North's government, although he had singled his independence earlier by resigning over his opposition to George III's Bill on Royal Marriages. A few months after this meeting he left North's government for the second time to become one of its strongest critics. Chatham and Fox were two of the most eloquent orators of the 18th century. They both proved to be America's greatest friends.

Review of the York Regiment.

Pub. as ye Act Directs Oct 14 1778 by W Richardson No 68 High Holborn

P. Carter Del.   T. Parson Sct

Anno Regni

GEORGII III.

REGIS

Magnæ Britanniæ, Franciæ, & Hiberniæ,

S E X T O.

At the Parliament begun and holden at *Westminster*,
the Nineteenth Day of *May*, *Anno Dom.* 1761,
in the First Year of the Reign of our Sovereign Lord *GEORGE* the Third, by the Grace
of God, of *Great Britain, France,* and *Ireland,*
King, Defender of the Faith, &c.

And from thence continued by several Prorogations to the
Seventeenth Day of *December*, 1765, being the Fifth Session
of the Twelfth Parliament of *Great Britain*.

G   **R**

L O N D O N:
Printed by *Mark Baskett*, Printer to the King's most Excellent
Majesty; and by the Assigns of *Robert Baskett*. 1766.

Review of the York Regiment
c. 1778

The Archbishop of York (dubbed by Horace Walpole as 'Archbishop Turpin', a well-known highwayman in Yorkshire) led the War Party and is presenting it to a doubting Britannia as a 'noble Corps, True and Staunch Friends to the Cause' and its leader declares, 'Please you Madam, for Mitres, Deaneries, and Prebendaries we will wade thro' an Ocean of Yanky Blood.' There are however two doubting soldiers on the left of the print who say the militant troops are 'neither true to God nor man' and they should all be hanged.

Independence spelt the end of the Anglican Church as no priest could be ordained without taking the Oath of Allegiance to the King, George III. Led by Maryland in 1776, colony after colony in 1777-78 disestablished the Church of England – Georgia, Virginia, North and South Carolina.

The Declaratory Act 1766

The passing of this Act, following the repeal of the Stamp Act, was a political blunder. The House of Commons could not retreat with grace, instead they insisted upon their supremacy. This act stated that Parliament 'had, hath, and of right ought to have full power and authority to make laws and statutes of sufficient form and validity to bind the colonies and people of America in all cases whatsoever.' The die was cast.

Engrav'd for the Westminster Magazine.

The Parricide.
A Sketch of Modern Patriotism.

The Parricide
1 May 1776
Westminster Magazine

This is a rare attack on opponents of George III's American policy. It accuses them of helping America to destroy Britain. Anger is directed against the so-called 'patriots': Chatham, Fox, Grafton – who is actually restraining Britannia's arm, Camden – who is muzzling the lion, and Wilkes – directing the dagger of the American Indian towards Britannia's heart. In America Wilkes had became a hero for standing up to and humiliating Parliament and the King. In the 1770s Wilkes tried to impeach those who had started the war and he must have welcomed the fact that the number 45, which referred to the famed issue No.45 of *The North Briton*, was worn by some patriots on their caps. On the 45th day of 1770, 45 New York Patriots ate 45 pounds of beefsteak from a bullock 45 months old. South Carolina even voted £1,500 (£98,000 in today's money) to pay off his debts. To America Wilkes was a fellow victim of royal tyranny.

Chapter Three

1773-1776
Boston

'Obstinate, undutiful and ungovernable'

ON 20 JANUARY 1774, London awoke to the startling news that on 16 December 1773 a band of Bostonians disguised as Mohawk Indians had boarded the three British vessels in the harbour – the *Dartmouth*, the *Eleanor* and the *Beaver* – that were carrying tea from the East India Company and had broken open 342 chests of tea throwing overboard 105,000lbs of tea, which would have made 24 million cups, with a value of over £10,000. This event, which had a comic aspect, had a huge political consequence, and it has passed into history as the Boston Tea Party.

Oxf. Mag. Sep. 1774.

BOREAS.

Æolus

I Promise to reduce the Americans.

Boreas – The Blind Trumpeter
September 1774
Oxford Magazine

Boreas was the Greek god of the north wind. This caricature appeared just before a general election, when North made a pledge, 'I Promise to reduce the Americans', that proved to be disastrous. Horace Walpole described North in his *Memoirs*:

'Nothing could be more coarse or clumsy or ungracious than his outside. Two large prominent eyes that rolled about to no purpose (for he was utterly short-sighted), a wide mouth, thick lips and inflated visage, gave him the air of a blind trumpeter. A deep untuneful voice which, instead of modulating, he enforced with unnecessary pomp, a total neglect of his person, and ignorance of every civil attention, disgusted all who judge by appearance, or without their approbation until it is courted. But within that rude casket were enclosed many useful talents. He had much wit, strong natural sense, assurance and promptness. What he did, he did without a mask, and was not delicate in choosing his means.'

Early in 1773, Lord North had been lobbied by the East India Company as it was in financial difficulties due to its warehouses in London being stacked to their roofs with tea it could not sell, largely as a result of merchants smuggling Dutch tea into America. North's seemingly ingenious plan was to allow the company to export the tea straight to America without any payment of colonial taxes in London. Once there, and with only 3d in the pound import duty to be met, it would undercut the smuggled Dutch tea – cheap tea for America must be popular. The House of Commons passed the Tea Act on 10 May with virtually no opposition as some leading Whigs had financial interests in the company.

The government expected no trouble since local protest about the tea duty had died away, and indeed for three months there was no reaction in America. The storm broke in October when news was leaked that the East India Company was going to ship some 500,000lbs of tea to Boston, New York, Philadelphia and Charleston. This would directly hit the existing legitimate tea merchants, and completely destroy the thriving and extensive trade of smuggling in Dutch tea, which was the basis of John Hancock's wealth. Thus the local economy of several states was threatened by the largest international company in the world and there was a fear that the tea monopoly would be extended to spices, drugs, chinaware, silks and calicos. It is indeed ironic that the American revolution was stirred to life by one of the first examples of globalisation.

A pamphlet, *The Alarm*, published in October 1773 and anonymously ascribed to Rusticus, asserted, 'Are we in like Manner to be given up to the Disposal of the East India Company, who have now the Assurance, to step forth in Aid of the Minister to execute his plan of enslaving America.'

Another consequence of the Tea Act was that the old cry of 'No taxation without representation' was resurrected: it was a propaganda coup for the anti-loyalists and gave them a cry for the streets. Boston was a tax-free haven and that was not going to be given up without a fight. Another inflammatory consequence was that the distribution of the East Indian tea in Massachusetts was given into the hands of a monopoly consisting of a few lucky loyalists, two of whom just happened to be the sons of Governor Hutchinson.

It was not just the tax issue – a good popular cry – but the deliberate attempt to interfere with the economic well-being of the colonists which turned the aggravation into open hostility in the coming months. At every port on the seaboard there was the threat of mob violence if British vessels docked to unload tea, leaving Boston as the only port prepared to accept them. It is therefore not surprising to find in the Declaration of Independence some three years later that one of the reasons for the resentment of British rule was 'a cutting-off of our trade in all parts of the world'.

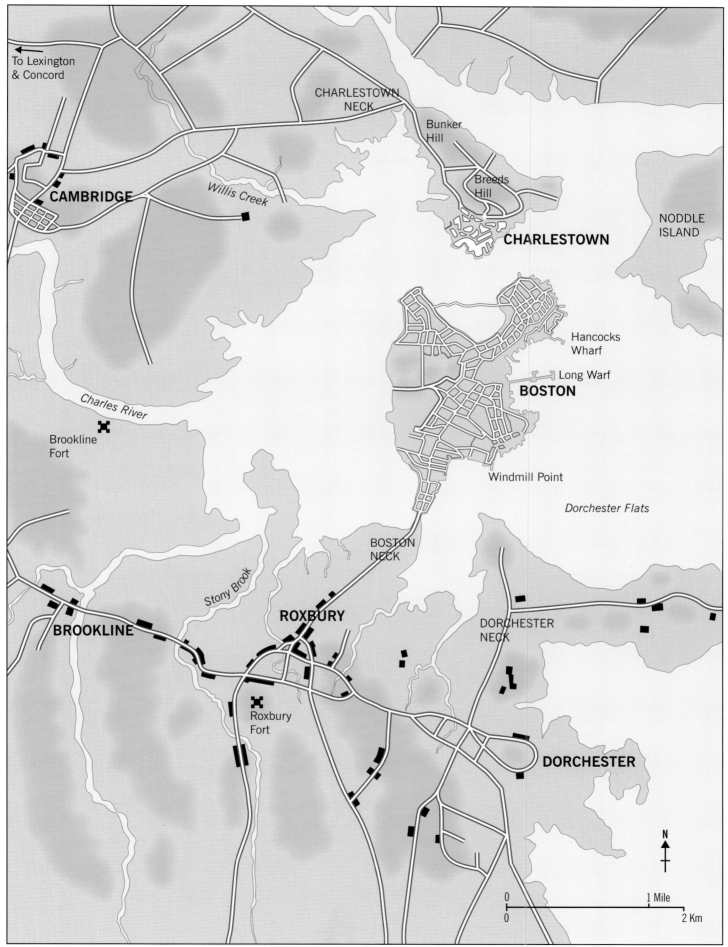

To Lexington
& Concord

CHARLESTOWN
NECK

Bunker
Hill

Breeds
Hill

CAMBRIDGE

Willis Creek

CHARLESTOWN

NODDLE
ISLAND

Hancocks
Wharf

Long Warf

BOSTON

Charles River

Brookline
Fort

Windmill Point

Dorchester Flats

BOSTON
NECK

Stony Brook

ROXBURY

DORCHESTER
NECK

BROOKLINE

Roxbury
Fort

DORCHESTER

N

0   1 Mile
0   2 Km

The able Doctor, or America Swallowing the Bitter Draught.

The Able Doctor, or America Swallowing the Bitter Draught
1 May 1774
London Magazine
This is the most famous print that paved the way to the war. North is forcing tea down America's throat which she spits back out into his face. In his pocket is a draft of the Boston Port Bill which was then before the House of Commons. The courtly clothes of Lord North contrast with the scantily-clad, bare-breasted figure of America: a contrast of the perceived civilisations. The print is an open attack upon the government's policy and Britannia holds her head in shame. Mansfield, the Lord Chief Justice who is never depicted favourably in prints, restrains America's arms while the lecherous Sandwich looks up her skirt. Bute is carrying a sword marked 'Military Law' while a Frenchman and a Spaniard ominously discuss the rich pickings they can make from the extraordinary conduct of the British government. Benjamin Franklin had observed early in 1770 that 'all Europe is attentive to the dispute'.

The Bostonians Paying the Excise-man – or –
Tarring and Feathering
31 October 1774
John Dawe, printed for Sayer and Bennett of Fleet Street, London
On 27 January 1774 John Malcomb, a Commissioner of Customs at Boston, had attempted to collect customs duties. A group of ruffians tarred and feathered him, led him to a gallows with a rope around his neck, and forced him to drink enormous quantities of tea. John Dawe, who had learnt his art and engraving from Hogarth, could not resist such a striking and comical event. In the background tea is being thrown into the harbour:

'For the Custom House Officers landing the Tea,
They Tarr'd him, and Feathr'd him, just as you see,
And they drench'd him so well both behind and before,
That he begg'd for God's sake, they would drench him no more.'

The Whitehall Pump.

The Whitehall Pump
1 May 1774

The Westminster Magazine

In this print the head of George III crowns the Whitehall Pump which is the source of the water Lord North is pouring over Britannia who is defending America represented by a Native Red Indian. The figures to the left include Mansfield and Sandwich. The protestors on the right are John Wilkes and Lord Camden who was a close friend of Chatham. The print reveals that there was considerable disquiet about the action which the government was taking against America. It also associates George III as being the *fons et origo* of the government's policy of repression.

Back in London there was little inkling of the explosive nature of the fuse that had been lit. In June Benjamin Franklin warned the government that 3d in the pound on tea 'is insufficient to overcome the patriotism of an American'. He was then publicly humiliated by the government who used the fact that he had privately caused to be printed a letter from Hutchinson, the Governor of Massachusetts, advocating sterner and harsher measures against the colonists which included a damning sentence, 'There must be an abridgment of what are called English Liberties'. Franklin was forced to appear before a meeting of privy counsellors where he was mercilessly and ruthlessly cross-examined by Wedderburn, the Solicitor General, who accused him of being a traitor. Franklin was stripped of a minor government post, but he was to have his revenge: years later on the day when the alliance between America and France was signed he wore the same suit of Manchester velvet that he had worn at his cross-examination.

North's government was not only surprised by the Boston Tea Party but it was shocked and appalled that such deliberate criminality had the support of most Bostonians. North decided, with the encouragement of the King, to punish Boston by

The Parl.^{mn} diffolvd, or,

The DEVIL turn'd FORTUNE TELLER.

The Parl.mn dissolved, or, The Devil turn'd Fortune Teller
September 1774

The Whimsical Repository

The devil as a fortune teller has conjured up an American Native Indian who is standing upon a prostrate British soldier while tapping upon a parliament building from which members are falling. Lord North and another peer are appalled at the prospect. Outside the window the heads on top of Temple Bar remind one of the Gate of Traitors.

closing the port of Boston and direct trade to Salem. This was particularly irksome as cargo offloaded in Salem had to be transferred to Boston in wagons. It was, however, the first of four acts known in American history as the Intolerable Acts, the Punitive Acts or the Coercive Acts: take your choice.

The second act was the Massachusetts Government Act which replaced elections for councillors with royal appointments and decreed that meetings of the freeholders and inhabitants – in effect the local government of the colony – could only be held with the governor's permission. The third was the Quartering Act which extended the powers of the governor to force residents to quarter British soldiers. This was to lead to the Third Amendment of the American Constitution which forbade quartering without the consent of the house-owner. The fourth act was the Administration of Justice Act which allowed the governor to decide whether and where a trial should take place. If any of the Boston Mohawks could be arrested they were to be tried at the Old Bailey in London, and the two leading colonial rebels, Sam Adams and John Hancock, headed the list.

On 16 April 1775 Gage received an order from London

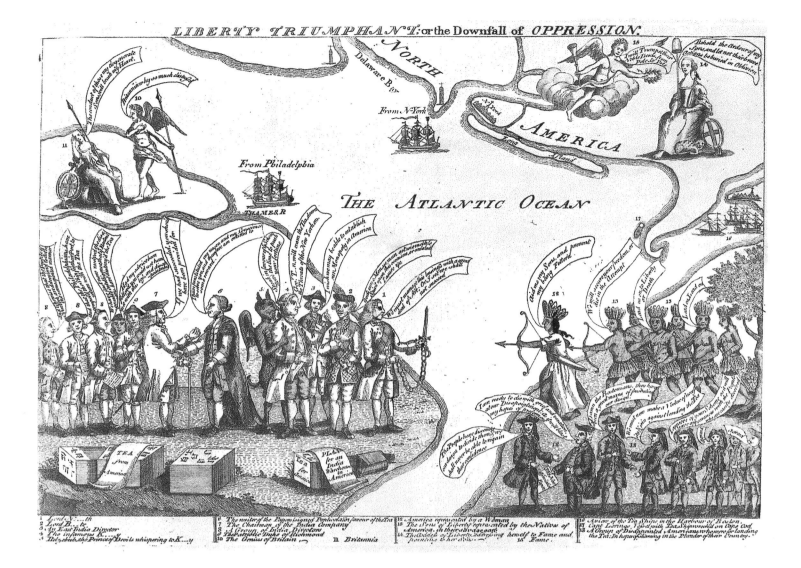

Liberty Triumphant – or – The Downfall of Oppression
Early 1774

This is a rare, important and well-informed print, which appeared in London, and which is very sympathetic to America and scornful of Britain, George III and his ministers. The Spirit of America, carrying the Cap of Liberty, proudly and confidently praises the 'Ardour of my Sons' while a despairing Britannia deplores 'The Conduct of these my degenerate Sons'. The villains on the left are the directors of the East India Company with their plans for a warehouse in America for their tea. Their alarm that their ships had been turned away from New York is being addressed by granting them a monopoly in Boston. The devil prompts George III to support North, 'Gov.r T---n will cram the Tea, down the Throats of the New Yorkers'. Americans are depicted as Native Red Indian braves, who tell their leader, a woman, 'Lead us to Liberty or Death'. The merchants who are standing below them are the lucky loyalists who would operate the monopoly, but even some of them are beginning to wonder whether they should change sides and stop the ships from unloading: already three are waiting in Boston harbour. There is no mention of the duty on tea for it was the disruption and distortion of regular trade that inflamed the Americans.

The Massachusetts Spy (opposite)
1774
Paul Revere

The main local paper carried in 1770 the first appearance of the symbol of Liberty holding the Cap of Liberty and on 7 July 1774 the editor, Isaiah Thomas, added the symbol of a rattlesnake, whose segments carry the initials of nine states, attacking a griffin that has the declaratory motto, 'Join or Die'. The snake device was first used by Benjamin Franklin in 1754 to urge the states to unite against the French and Native Red Indians.

with which he did not agree: to arrest the members of the illegal Provincial Congress which was meeting at Concord some twenty-one miles from Boston. The colonial executive power was challenged and being superseded by self-appointed American bodies. In September 1774 the Continental Congress met in Philadelphia for the first time, and the Massachusetts Provincial Congress had chosen Concord as the seat of its government. Gage also knew from spies in that small town that there were stores of guns, gunpowder and three 24-pounder cannons which had a range of 1,500 yards and could clearly threaten Boston and its shipping channels. Sam Adams, who had been for a long time an agent provocateur in undermining British rule and reputation, may well have been in contact with the French over these cannons. He is certainly known to have burnt many letters before he fled from Concord.

Back in Boston, the rebel townspeople came to know that troops were being moved secretly on the night of 18th April. Two lanterns hung in the tower of Boston North Church: one being lit was the signal that the redcoats were marching out across the Boston Neck to Lexington; and two being lit that they would take a shorter route probably by boat through Charlestown. Two lanterns were lit that night and militia in the countryside were aroused for the British army was on the march. Paul Revere, one of the Sons of Liberty and an excellent horseman, rode out with the news to Lexington and rode also into history. Such is the mixture of romance and myth that surrounds the start of this war.

When Sam Adams heard Paul Revere's news he persuaded Captain John Parker of the Lexington Militia to form a line of 70 militia men across the common to check the redcoats. This was bound to lead to an exchange of gunfire and when Adams heard the first shot – no one knew who fired first – he cheerfully exclaimed, 'Oh what a glorious morning this is for America'.

The British troops forced the militia to flee, killing seven, while only one redcoat was slightly wounded. The men had fired without the order of their officer, Major Pitcairn, who was furious, but the damage had been done. A small force of 600 men then went on to Concord, just two miles away, seized the cannons and other weapons but most of the arms had been spirited away or buried. By then the whole countryside had been raised and hundreds of militiamen rallied to the north of Concord, alarmed when they saw some buildings burning in the town. The redcoats took up a position on the bridge, but when they were faced by 400 rebels, shots were exchanged and as they were running out of ammunition the only option was to retreat to Boston. They had been in Concord for just four hours.

The British troops then realised they were in a trap and recent historical research has argued that the whole episode was a cleverly planned ambush to lure the British into Concord, to force an engagement, and to punish them on the inevitable retreat to Boston. The whole area around Boston had been alarmed by what the British intended to do – earlier Gage had warned Lord North that 'the whole country is in arms and motion'.

For over a year tension had been rising across Massachusetts: seditious handbills circulated; redcoats were hissed in the streets; and farmers, shopkeepers, blacksmiths and merchants met together in the villages in minute-men companies, which were de facto local militias. The redcoats were looked upon as an occupying force compelling obedience to a distant country, a stubborn king, and a corrupt government which among other things wanted to prevent them expanding westwards. The rebels saw that their very way of life was threatened and they rallied to that cause. Most were farmers and were therefore excellent shots. Along the winding road that led back to Boston the militia guerrillas struck time and time again – from the hills and behind walls, boulders, trees and barns they fired upon the retreating column. British officers had to stop the troops fleeing in panic before they reached Lexington. There they were reinforced by a rescue column led by Lord Percy, but even he lost 36 men from the Royal Welch Fusiliers who were covering the retreat.

The British army for the first time realised what they were up against – five thousand militiamen had turned out and they even had a leader, a farmer, Brigadier Heath. They were also alarmed to find as they were leaving Concord, a dead British soldier who had been scalped.

The whole operation was a humiliation – British casualties were 73 killed, 174 wounded. The rebel losses were 49 killed, 39 wounded. The most successful army of the most successful country had been outwitted and outgunned. The propaganda machine of the rebels went into overdrive – women and children were in danger from 'the butchery hands of an inhuman soldiery'.

Another propaganda coup was that the news of the engagements arrived in London on 26 May from a report received by the agent of the Massachusetts Company. This had been carried on a faster schooner than the official report from Gage which arrived on 10 June. The government had first dismissed the American report as false or exaggerated but within two weeks they had to accept the truth. George III's reaction was that England would ensure that her 'rebellious children rue the hour they cast off obedience'.

George Washington, who later in the year was to become the Commander-in-Chief of this militia army, recognised that Concord had changed everything – 'unhappy it is, though, to reflect that a brother's sword has been sheathed in a brother's breast, and that the once happy and peaceful plains of America are either to be drenched with blood, or inhabited by slaves. Sad alternative! But can a virtuous man hesitate in his choice?'

In May Gage received more reinforcements, together with three generals: Howe, Clinton and Burgoyne. Howe was clearly the Commander-in-Chief in waiting and he decided that the reputation of the British army had to be retrieved, particularly as rebel forces were now gathering in strength on the mainland circling Boston. The Charlestown Peninsula was just to the north across the channel and like the city itself was connected to the mainland by a narrow peninsula. Gage had abandoned a redoubt on the peninsula and rebel troops had taken possession, establishing a position on the two hills, Breeds Hill and Bunker Hill.

Howe's troops, some 2,300 strong, landed by sea and advanced up Breeds Hill. They were met with withering fire and failed to take the hill. Howe then decided to lead his men from the front, an act of foolhardy courage, which led to all of his personal staff either being killed or wounded. Running out of ammunition the rebels could not withstand the sheer force of numbers and abandoned Breeds Hill and Bunker Hill, but falling back in an orderly way they gained the mainland. The British should have pursued them but they had lost too many officers and sergeants to lead them further. This was the first time that Howe was to fail to push home his advantage to crush the rebel army. Bunker Hill was a pyrrhic victory: 140 Americans dead; 271 wounded; 228 British dead; 826 wounded. It was a disaster for the British. Howe reported that he had lost 90 officers and one British officer, Major Sill, lamented that 'the shocking carnage of that day never will be out of my mind till the day of my death'.

Nine day's later Gage wrote a despatch to the Secretary of State which really served as his epitaph:

'These people show a spirit and courage against us they never showed against the French…They are now spirited up by a rage and enthusiasm as great as ever people were possessed of, and you must proceed in earnest or give the business up. A small body acting in one place will not avail. You must have large armies, making diversions on different sides, to divide their forces. The loss we have sustained is greater than we can bear.'

A New Method of Macarony Making, as practised at Boston
12 October 1774

This mezzotint shows a customs officer being tarred and feathered by two Bostonians: one with a cockade in his hat as a sign of liberty, and the other wears a hat with '45' inscribed on it reminding everyone of Wilkes' attack upon the monarchy in the 45th edition of *The North Briton*. The customs officer is going to be made to drink tea and he seems to have only just escaped a hanging.

The Tar Brush as a weapon of intimidation was a unique American invention. The threat of it could "persuade" British colonial officials not to implement, not to collect, and not to enforce. The more senior could also be harried by being hanged in effigy, and if that failed Sam Adams could muster a mob cleverly not armed with cutlasses or muskets, but clubs and axes. This led the tea commissioners in New York and Philadelphia to recognise that if tea was to be unloaded in their ports, then mob violence would follow.

The Bostonians in Distress (opposite)
19 November 1774

This mezzotint is sympathetic to the distress suffered by the Bostonians as a result of the cessation of their trade. They are suspended in a cage from the Liberty Tree – the rallying point for patriots. Ironically the tree was cut down for fuel when the British blockaded Boston during the winter of 1775-76. In the summer General Gage had ordered regiments of foot soldiers and artillery to be sent to Boston. They had camped on the narrow strip of ground called Boston Neck which connected Boston to the mainland in preparation for the siege. The men in the boats are offering fish to the Bostonians. A minister laments while another prisoner pushes out papers marked 'Policies'. The engraver was clearly familiar with some practices in America as slaves convicted of capital offences in the colonies were held in cages and left to starve to death. The cage became a symbol of slavery and barbarity.

The Congress – or – The Necessary Politicians

On 20 October 1774 the Congress in America passed its famous Resolutions which demanded a boycott of British trade and goods. They were widely printed in Britain. In this Tory bog-house one man wipes his arse with the Resolutions while another reads Dr Johnson's pamphlet supporting the Government, *Taxation No Tyranny*, which was published in February 1775. The print on the wall depicts Chatham, America's friend, as being tarred and feathered.

THE ALTERNATIVE OF WILLIAMS BURG.

Plate IV.

London Printed for R. Sayer & J. Bennett No 53 Fleet Street as the Act directs 16 Feb. 1775

A Society of Patriotic Ladies at Edentown in North Carolina
14 February 1775
John Dawe, printed for Sayer and Bennett of Fleet Street, London

In this mezzotint, an elderly battleaxe in Carolina persuades her lady friends to sign a petition to boycott English goods including tea, for that is what they have been asked to do by the resolution of the Continental Congress in 1774. 'We, the Ladys of Edentown do hereby Solemnly Engage not to Conform to that Pernicious Custom of Drinking Tea or that we the aforesaid Ladys will not promote any Manufacture from England until such time that All Acts which tend to Enslave this our Native Country shall be repealed.' On the left three ladies tip the contents of tea caddies into a man's hat and on the right a dog pisses on another tea caddy. The boycott was used as a weapon against British commerce and it involved ordinary people – carpenters refused to build barracks in Boston; tailors offered a cheaper price for clothes made from American cloth; and in 1769 Carolina banned the export of tanned leather as no new saddlery or shoes were to be imported. British exports were hit – a frying-pan-maker in Birmingham was left with several tonnes.

The Alternative of Williamsburg (opposite)
16 February 1775
John Dawe, printed for Sayer and Bennett of Fleet Street, London

The citizens of Virginia were required to sign either the Association or the Resolutions passed by the Williamsburg Convention in August 1774. Loyalists are being threatened by men with clubs and by a butcher with a knife to sign-up. *The Chronicle* of 26 January 1774 reported that when Virginians were reluctant 'a gibbett' was erected in the capital, Williamsburg, from which was hung a barrel of tar and a barrel of feathers, each inscribed 'A Cure for the Refractory' which proved very effective in securing signatures. One of the Resolutions of Williamsburg stated that 'Every exporter of Tobacco should be considered as an enemy to the community' – British pipe smokers were to suffer!

Battle of Lexington
1775
Ralph Earl

This is a contemporary engraving by Ralph Earl who was not present at the skirmish but visited the town a few days later to collect the details. He states clearly that it was the British force that fired first, though this was disputed. He also indicates that a British officer was ordering his men to fire which was not the case. Major Pitcairn was so appalled that he rode out in front of the men to stop them firing. His official report stated:

> *'Without my order or regularity, the light infantry began scattered fire and continued in that situation for some little time, contrary to the repeated orders of both me and the officers that were present.'*

Lieutenant John Barker of the King's Own Regiment passed on the blame to his men 'who were so wild they could hear no orders'.

1. Major Pitcairn, at the head of the
2. The Party, who first fired on the
3. Part of the Provincial Company

ttle of Lexington, April 19th 1775. Plate I.

A. Doolittle. Sculp.

4. Regular Companies on the road to Concord.
5. The Metinghouse at Lexington.
6. The Public Inn.

r Granadiers.
s at Lexington.
ington.

The Battle of Concord
19 April 1775
Amos Doolittle

Amos Doolittle, a self-taught engraver, was a member of the militia which had camped near Boston for weeks. He was not present in Concord on the famous day but he visited it shortly afterwards accompanied by another artist soldier, Ralph Earl. They recreated the drama of the conflict and had a set of four engravings on sale by Christmas. In this one the Commander of the British force, Colonel Smith, is viewing the land with Major Pitcairn who became something of a hero, even with Americans, as he had tried to stop his men firing at Lexington and later he was to die a courageous soldier's death at Bunker Hill. These prints, which exaggerated the orderly redcoat army and the sheer number of their massed columns, were powerful weapons in the propaganda war.

View of the Town of Concord.

marching into Concord. 4 & 5 Colonel Smith & Major Pitcairn viewing the Provincials
drawn up in order. who were mustering on an East Hill in Concord.
the Provincial Stores 6. The Townhouse. 7 The Meetinghouse.

A. Doolittle Sculpt

The Battle of Concord – The North Bridge
Amos Doolittle, Plate 3

In Concord British troops searched barns, houses, stores and even the jail where Major Pitcairn held a pistol to the head of the jailer to persuade him to open the doors. They eventually found and destroyed the cannon which 'peace-loving farmers should have no truck with'. The column then stopped at the North Bridge when they were faced by a column of militiamen who had formed up on the other side. The rebels had seen fires in the town and had feared for the townsfolk. The British on the other hand did not want their return to Boston to be cut off by this force which had appeared almost from nowhere. Shots were exchanged – the war had begun.

The Retreat (following page)
19 April 1775

The column retreating from Concord under Colonel Smith was saved at Lexington by the relief column of 1,200 men that had been sent out from Boston under the command of Lord Percy, who is at the bottom right of the print. He was a professional soldier who had mapped the roads of Massachusetts. Smith knew that he was saved when a cannon ball from one of Percy's guns crashed through the Meeting House in Lexington. Percy also burnt three houses and despatched flanking parties to root out and kill any rebels. Lieutenant MacKenzie of the Royal Welch Fusiliers recorded in his diary, 'many houses were plundered by the soldiers, not withstanding the efforts of the officers to prevent it. I have no doubt that this has inflamed the rebels.' In this print one file of men carrying bags say, 'Away with your plunder'; another says, 'I'll run for what's in this box will be the making of me.' It was only Percy's brilliant retreat from Lexington that saved the redcoats from being overwhelmed by the growing number of militias. Percy had a high regard for them, 'Whoever looks upon them as an irregular mob will find himself much mistaken: they have men amongst them who having been employed as rangers against the Indians and the Canadians; and this country being much covered with wood and hilly is very advantageous for their method of fighting.'

gement at the North Bridge in Concord.

...rs who fired first   2. The Provincials headed by Colonel Robinson &   A. Doolittle Sculp.
...Bridge   Major Buttrick. 3 The Bridge

The SCOTCH BUTCHERY, Boston. 1775.

The Scotch Butchery, Boston 1775

Mansfield and Bute are the 'Super Intendants of the Butchery/from the two great Slaughter Houses'. At this time Bute had no influence over either the King or the government but he is featured in many prints for many still believed he held influence through the backstairs. The other two figures in the centre of the print also come from Scotland: Wedderburn, the Solicitor General, and Colonel Simon Fraser who had commanded a regiment of Scottish troops against the French in the Seven Years War. On the outbreak of hostilities with America Fraser raised a new regiment, the 78th Fraser Highlanders. Scots from the Highlands had the reputation of being the fiercest, most brutal part of the British army and here they even seem to strike terror into other British troops who throw down their arms.

Boston was Britain's nemesis. The Boston Tea Party was the provocative act that led to war: Lexington, Concord and Bunker Hill were the first disasters and there was no speedy attempt to destroy the ramshackle rebel army. The siege of Boston by American forces lasted from the summer of 1775 to the spring of 1776, and it ended with Britain's humiliating evacuation of the port – the first major victory for America. The long siege allowed George Washington, who had not had any military experience for fifteen years, to grow accustomed to command, and to fashion an army from the 'rabble in arms': the inexperienced, untrained, ill-equipped, ill-disciplined volunteers whom the states sent to him. Washington's personal views on his troops in 1775 included: 'A dirty mercenary spirit pervades the whole'.

Washington's commanders, Nathanael Greene, Henry Knox, and Israel Putnam known as 'Old Put', learnt how to work together, and cooled Washington's ardour for a frontal assault on Boston. The daring expedition under Knox – who had previously been a bookseller in Maine, and brought the 58 mortars and cannon which had been abandoned at Fort Ticonderoga, 300 miles distant at Lake Champlain – showed that the Americans knew much more about their country than the British. It was a tremendous boost for morale and Knox

An Exact View of The Late Battle at Charlestown June 17th 1775

An Exact View of The Late Battle at Charlestown, June 17th 1775

This was America's first victory in the war. In early 1775, Howe despatched Clinton with a force of 3,000 men to open up a campaign in the Carolinas and seize the important port of Charleston. He would be joined there by Lord Cornwallis who was sailing from Dublin in a fleet under the command of Admiral Peter Parker. Fort Sullivan protected the entrance to the harbour and Clinton, who had not reconnoitred the land, landed his force in June on Long Island hoping to ford the channel to Fort Sullivan. He found that the channel was seven foot deep and so he had to withdraw leaving it to Parker to bombard Charleston into submission. General Lee had been appointed as the commander but the real victor was a militia captain, Colonel Moultrie, who although he had only 61 cannons to 230 held off the attack from the British fleet. He was helped by the bar in the harbour which kept some of the heavy hitting vessels out-of-range and on which three vessels managed to beach, and also by Fort Sullivan's thick walls of logs made from a spongy Palmetto filled with sand and clay which simply absorbed the shells. Within a few days Clinton decided to return to New York; Lee's reputation soared, but the unsung hero was Colonel Moultrie and his victory had a huge strategic importance since Charleston was to remain the major supply port to the rebellion up until 1780.

wrote to his wife, 'We shall cut no small figure through the country with our cannon.' The guns from Ticonderoga reached Boston in January and by 4 March – to the utter astonishment of the British – they were moved brilliantly overnight onto the Dorchester Heights which commanded Boston and meant the town was now at the mercy of American cannon fire. What the British did not know was that Washington had no bombs for the mortars and was very short of powder. On 9 March Howe ordered the evacuation of the town, and on 18 March Washington entered with flags flying and drums beating – the 'lobster backs' were gone.

Gage and Howe disastrously allowed themselves to be besieged in Boston for nine months. The population dropped from 17,000 to 5,000 as many families favouring the rebels sold up and left. It was not only gruelling – a shortage of fresh provisions left the troops subsisting on salt pork and peas – but it was also a period of limited, negative and frustrating campaigning. They were not prepared to break out through the American lines, risking another Bunker Hill, and they lived in the hope that the American troops would simply disappear during the long winter: they didn't. Boston should have been abandoned earlier and the war taken to the Americans. It was a very bad start to King George's war.

April 4. 1775

1. One String Jack Deliver your Property
2. Begar Just so en France? Accomplices
3. Te Deum
4. I Give you that man's money for my use

5..... I will not be Robbed
6..... I shall be wounded with you
7...... I am Blinded
8...... The French Roman Catholick Town of Quebeck
9..... The English Protestant Town of Boston

Price 6.

The Pit Prepared for Others

Virtual Representation, 1775

This is an interesting print since America is not depicted as a Native Indian but a respectable, well-dressed, portly figure brandishing a stick declaring, 'I will not be Robbed'. Bute is firing a blunderbuss but this time he has allies – the Speaker of the House of Commons with his Mace and, behind him, a French courtier and a priest. They are fair-weather friends: quite happy to still their natural hostility to Britain while the Quebec Act which sanctioned Roman Catholicism for Canada was passing through Parliament.

Britannia blindfolded is rushing into the Pit of Perdition. Boston, the English Protestant town, is in flames while Montreal enjoys peace and prosperity.

Noddle-Island or How are we decieved (opposite)
12 May 1776
M Darly

After the skirmishes at Lexington and Concord in April 1775, the first battle of the war was fought on the outskirts of Boston at Bunker Hill in June 1775. The British won but with an appalling loss of dead and wounded. General Gage was replaced as commander-in-chief by Sir William Howe.

George Washington with 15,000 men reinforced the siege of Boston, seized Dorchester Heights, and trained his cannons upon the city. On 4 March 1776 Howe had to evacuate Boston. Four months later the Declaration of Independence was passed.

The print satirises the defeat: Noddle Island was another name for William Island in Boston harbour. The title contains a pun on Howe's name and a reference to a misleading account given in the official *London Gazette*. Walpole wrote, 'nobody was deceived'. The two armies fight it out in the elaborate coiffure.

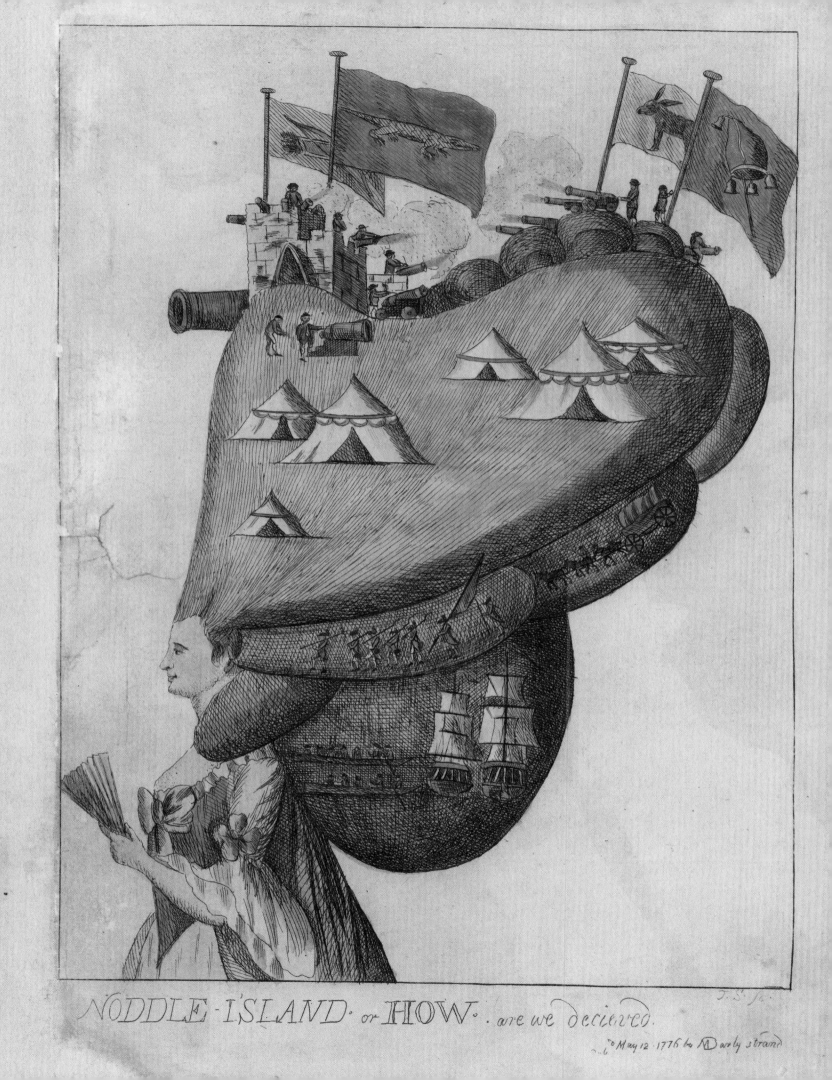

NODDLE·I'SLAND· or HOW· ·are we decieved·

To May 12·1776 by MDarly strand

The Battle of Bunker Hill

This portrayal of the battle by Winthrop Chandler (1747-1790), the Colonial-era painter, was probably painted in 1776. The British troops ferried across from Boston are in the foreground advancing up Breeds Hill which the Americans are just holding. This view emphasises the dominant power of the British forces: they commanded the sea, Boston itself, and at this time they outnumbered the American rebels.

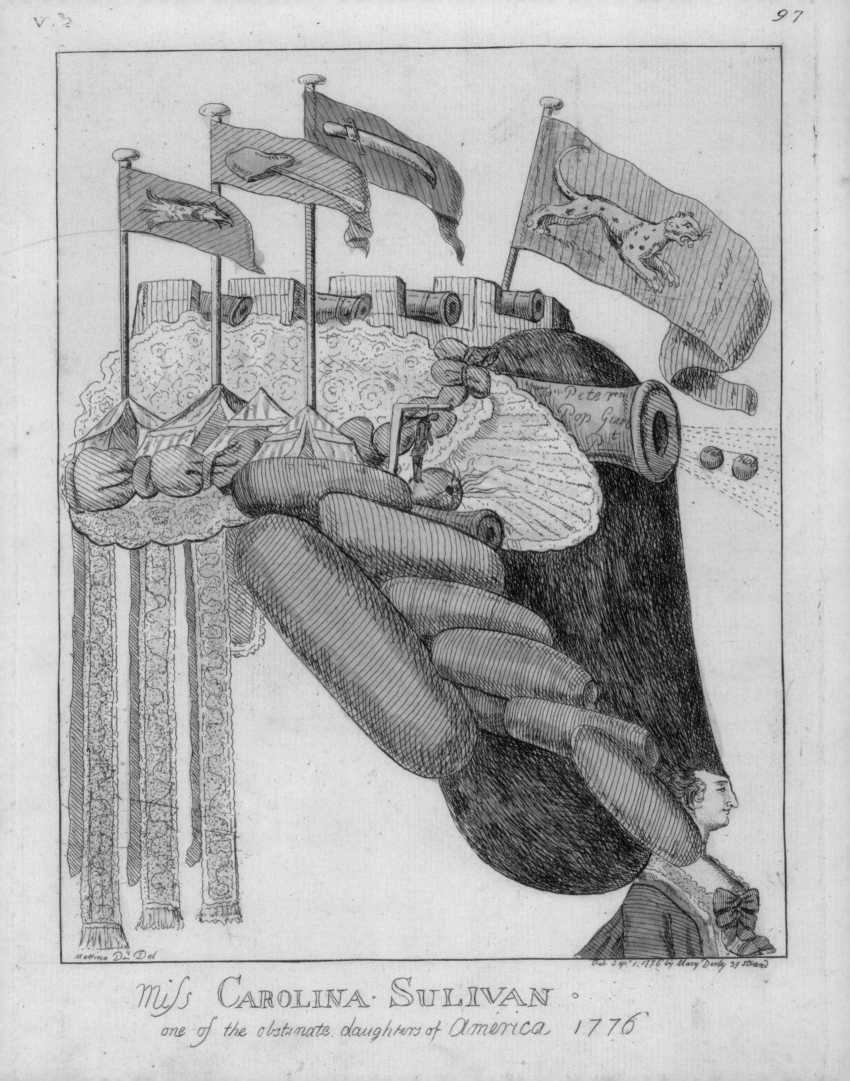

Mattina Dr. Del

Pub. Sep. 1. 1776 by Mary Darly 39 Strand

Miss CAROLINA SULIVAN .

one of the obstinate daughters of America 1776

Miss Carolina Sulivan one of the obstinate daughters of America

M Darly

This is how Mary Darly, the London engraver, reflected on the Battle of Charleston. The curls of the lady's hair are transformed into the wall of Palmetto logs. The cannon in the print bears the name 'Peter Pop Gun', possibly a pun on the British Admiral Peter Parker. The governors of Virginia, North and South Carolina and Georgia had hoped to raise bands of loyalists to support the British troops, but their hopes were dashed. The rebels won at Moore's Creek Bridge in North Carolina and the loyalists were routed at Great Bridge in Virginia.

Chapter Four

New York and New Jersey 1776

'Dear General, we are fleeing before the British.' Joseph Reed, Washington's secretary

WITHIN DAYS THE VARIOUS REGIMENTS in the American rebel army left Boston and marched towards New York which John Adams had described as 'a kind of key to the whole continent'. Whoever controlled New York controlled the Hudson River thus separating the rebels in New England from those in the south. But unlike Boston there were many more loyalists – half of the New York Chamber of Commerce was loyalists and two-thirds of the property belonged to Tories. Washington arrived on 13 April and established his headquarters at No.1 Broadway, a fine mansion on the tip of Manhattan. He set about planning its defence against an invasion with a force that barely amounted to 10,000 men. One of his most respected generals, Charles Lee, who had once served as an officer in the British army held the view that without command of the sea New York could not be held. Washington did not have a navy but the British could muster a fleet of over 250 ships.

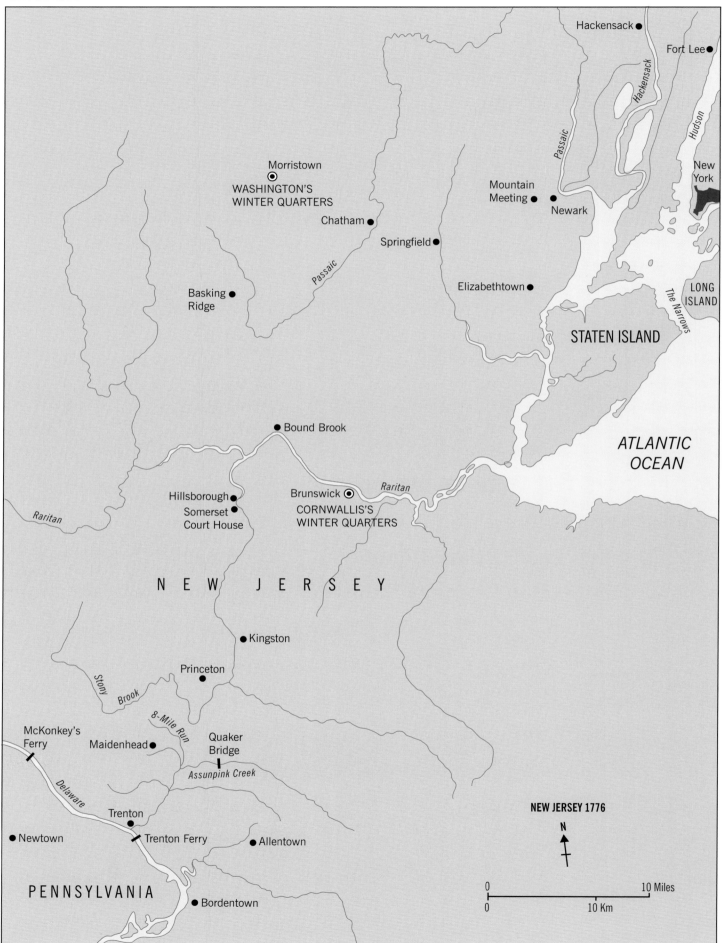

Hackensack

Fort Lee

Hackensack

Passaic

Hudson

New York

Morristown
WASHINGTON'S
WINTER QUARTERS

Mountain
Meeting

Newark

Chatham

Springfield

Basking
Ridge

Passaic

Elizabethtown

LONG
ISLAND

The Narrows

STATEN ISLAND

*ATLANTIC
OCEAN*

Bound Brook

Hillsborough

Somerset
Court House

Brunswick

Raritan

CORNWALLIS'S
WINTER QUARTERS

Raritan

N E W   J E R S E Y

Kingston

Princeton

Stony

Brook

8-Mile Run

McKonkey's
Ferry

Maidenhead

Quaker
Bridge

Assunpink Creek

Delaware

NEW JERSEY 1776

N

Trenton

Newtown

Trenton Ferry

Allentown

PENNSYLVANIA

Bordentown

0   10 Miles

0   10 Km

On 2 July the British landed on Staten Island, just south of New York. Two days later the Continental Congress in Philadelphia voted to declare Independence for America and published its famous Declaration. For the rebels there was no going back and the war was given a great purpose: the creation of a new country – the United States of America – as John Adams wrote, 'We are in very midst of a revolution'. The Declaration was read out in public in New York on 9 July and a mob rushed to Bowling Green to pull down the great gilt equestrian statue of George III and cut off its head – shades of Saddam Hussein in 2003.

To THE P U B L I C.

Before launching his invasion of New York Howe, in his role as Peace Commissioner, sent a letter to 'George Washington Esq.' which was rejected as 'not known at this address'. Ambrose Searle, Howe's secretary, was amazed at Washington's 'vanity and insolence' to claim the rank of general. It was only when Washington was recognised as a general that they could meet. But peace overtures were futile. Throughout July and August, scores of British ships arrived in the waters lying between Staten Island and Brooklyn. On 22 August 4,000 redcoats, in a brilliant amphibious operation, were landed on the southern coast of Long Island that led up to Brooklyn. Within days their number had increased to 15,000 with an additional 5,000 Hessians. The British army was faced by 12,000 rebels spread along the Brooklyn Heights. Clinton personally reconnoitred the land and found an unguarded pass on the right flank through which he passed with 10,000 men threatening to roll-up the American positions.

This led to the first British victory of the war at Flatbush (later known as the Battle of Brooklyn) where the Americans were not simply defeated, but routed. Howe reported 3,300 Americans killed and 1,097 captured including two generals: his own losses were 39 killed and 267 wounded with the Hessians losing only 5. The remainder of the American army fled to the last defensive positive, the Brooklyn Lines, expecting another assault but once again Howe hesitated and held back for three days.

Washington dithered but then decided to move the remnants of his army back over the East River. He was helped by the wind and weather which prevented English ships sailing northwards, so the transfer of men was conducted successfully in one night: the first of Washington's many retreats over a river – over the next three months he was to retreat over 170 miles. One British soldier recorded that, 'The rebels flee like scared rabbits'. With a better, more-inspired leader with a killer instinct, the British could have put paid to the Continental Army and

even possibly the American rebellion on 28 August.

Washington failed to realise that holding New York against a professional army that had total command of the Hudson and East Rivers was impossible. This was the advice of Nathanael Greene: 'A speedy retreat is absolutely necessary.' He also recommended burning the city but when Congress demurred Washington observed, 'Had it been left to the dictates of my own judgment New York would have been laid in ashes.' But his next tactics were exactly the same as those that failed in Brooklyn: he put his men on hills he believed could be held - Harlem Heights and to the north of New York, White Plains: both had to be abandoned under British assaults. Then he tried to hold the two forts on either side of the Hudson River – Fort Washington in Manhattan and Fort Lee in New Jersey. He should have ordered a general evacuation but instead it was decided to hold Fort Washington which was thought to be impregnable. It fell to the Hessians and 2,837 Americans had to march between two lines of these German soldiers to lay down their arms and enter captivity. When the news of the fall of New York reached England, Josiah Wedgwood recorded the surge in patriotic fervour, 'Our people at Newcastle went wild with joy'. Perhaps it would be over by Christmas.

By October 1776 Washington, then in New Jersey, had a much depleted force and many cannons and field guns had been abandoned. He had seen his large army fall to just 2,000 fighting men, mostly Virginians. By 20 November British generals had captured 4,400 rebels. General Lee brought an additional 3,000 New Englanders but Washington was further disappointed that

The Suppression of Free Speech
20 April 1775
New York Gazetteer

The colonial government's case did not go by default. Jemmy Rivington was the editor of the *New York Gazetteer* which had the largest circulation in the colonies – 3,600 subscribers in October 1774. He dubbed the Whig newspaper, the *Boston Gazette*, 'Monday's Dung Barge', and the *Massachusetts Spy* that 'Boston Snake of Sedition'. A mob hanged him in effigy on 13 April 1775 at New Brunswick and in reply he published this image of himself being hanged for the defence of a free press. This was too much and early in May a mob attacked his house and printery, and he had to seek safety on a British ship. Later another marauding party took away all his lead type. There was no room for dissent in the land of the brave and the free.

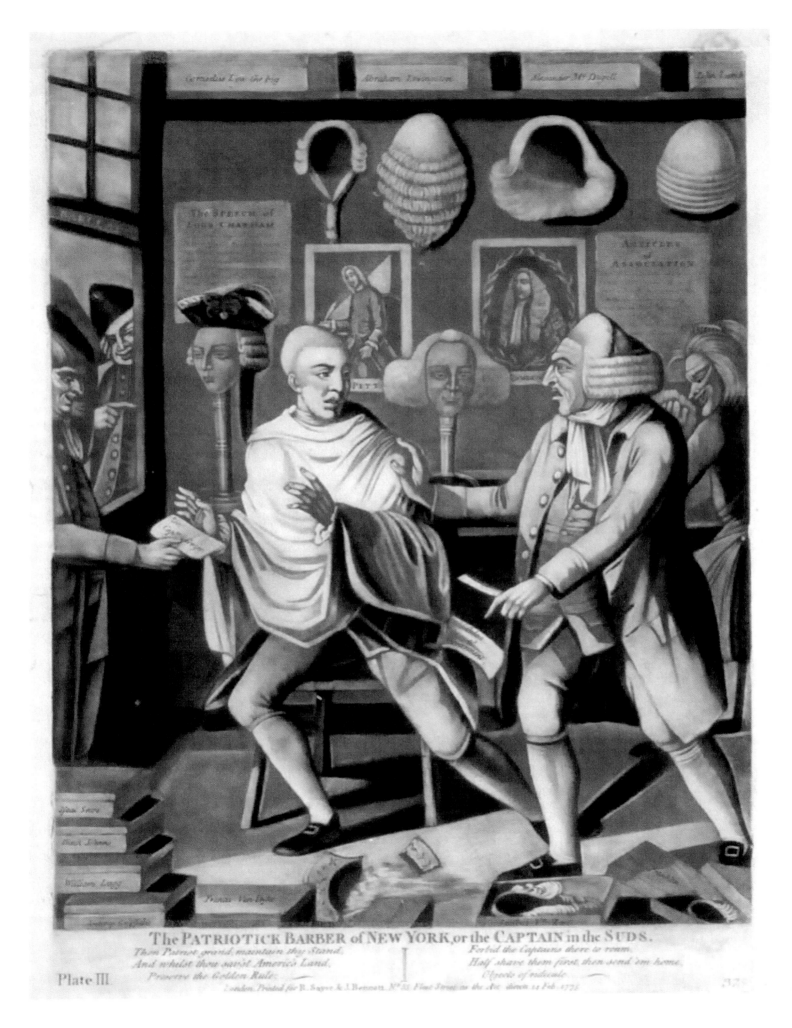

The PATRIOTICK BARBER of NEW YORK, or the CAPTAIN in the SUDS.

Then Patriot grand, maintain thy Stand,
And whilst thou sav'st Americ's Land,
Preserve the Golden Rule.

Forbid the Captains there to roam,
Half shave them first, then send 'em home,
Objects of ridicule.

Plate III.

London, Printed for R. Sayer & J. Bennett, N.º 53 Fleet Street as the Act directs 12 Feb. 1775.

General Grant
An engraving by the Scottish caricaturist John Kay

General Grant, a former Governor of Florida, was a fat, bellicose, gastronome who took on his campaigns his own black cook, Baptiste. His comments on the crushing defeat of the Americans at the Battle of Brooklyn, September 1776, were:

'You will be glad that we have had the field day I talked of in my last letter. If a good bleeding can bring these Bible-faced Yankees to their senses, the fever of independency should soon abate.'

In 1778 when Clinton was ordered to send men to the West Indies to withstand French attacks, Grant was despatched there with ten regiments.

The Patriotick Barber of New York, or the Captain in the Suds
14 February 1775
Phillip Dawe, printed by Sayer and Bennett of Fleet Street, London

When Jacob Vrendenburgh, a barber in Barclay Street, New York, discovered that his customer was Captain John Crozer, Commander to the *Empress of Russia*, a British ship in the river, he refused to finish shaving him. This incident was circulated on a card by the Sons of Liberty in October 1774 and news of it appeared in the *Kentish Gazette* on 7 January 1775. On the wall there are pictures of Chatham, the champion of America, and Camden, an ardent opponent of the Stamp Act. Alongside them are the Articles of Association passed by Congress on 2 October 1774 binding their constituents to boycotting British goods. The wig boxes on the floor bear the names of leading New York politicians: Alexander McDougall 'the American Wilkes', the radical John Lamb, Isaac Sears, Griffiths and Van Dyke, Sons of Liberty, and Livingstone and Franklin, who were later to be active fighters in the war. It is clear that political commentators at the time followed events in America very closely and had a sense of foreboding about what was going to happen.

just 500 came from Pennsylvania and Philadelphia could raise only 1,500.

In those months of October, November and December, Howe could have pursued and destroyed the rebel army. In his defence it is said that he was trying to reach an accommodation which the Americans would be willing to accept because he realised that it would be impossible to conquer and control America with a British army, since no force could be large enough to undertake that role. Howe's war aim was not total submission achieved by an overwhelming defeat; instead he hoped to reduce the fighting capacity of the rebels to force them to seek terms. He misjudged their determination.

Washington's tactics were no better than Howe's. There was an alternative advocated by Arthur Lee, his second-in-command and one of the shrewdest strategists. Lee and Gates, another ex-British officer, knew it was impossible to fashion from the rebels a professional field army capable of taking on the British in a set battle. They preferred guerrilla attacks, 'a cloud of mosquitoes', using local militias to surprise and harass the British forces and so sap their morale and undermine their ability to control the vast area of 13 states. Lee also advocated a scorched earth policy – it is not surprising that he was called 'a reckless, unstable, untrustworthy adventurer', but he was unable to implement his strategy since he was captured in December 1776 while eating his breakfast, wearing his dressing gown, at a tavern in a village appropriately called Basking Ridge, separated from his troops. He was not released until 1778.

Washington retreated over the Hackensack, Passaic and Raritan rivers while Cornwallis moved south to establish a British forward base at New Brunswick on the road to Philadelphia. Washington was then at his weakest – on 1 December 2,000 militia troops from New Jersey and Maryland decided just to walk away from the war and go home. This led him to retreat further to the small town of Trenton – a staging post on the road to Philadelphia in New Jersey on the River

Delaware which marked the boundary with the state of Pennsylvania. He was lucky that Cornwallis, who was not a sufficiently flexible and quick-witted field commander, paused after taking Brunswick for six days. Furthermore many of the citizens of New Jersey who hitherto had only been lukewarm supporters of the rebels became devoted patriots following the extensive looting by the British and Hessian troops. Nonetheless Washington decided to move his army across the Delaware to the greater safety of Pennsylvania.

On 13 December Howe made one of the most fateful decisions of the war when he suspended military operations until the spring: the warm comforts of New York beckoned. For the third time the rebel army had been let off the hook, but it was that army and its leader Washington which were the only force that could secure the continued independence of the United States. The British occupation of towns like New York and Philadelphia did not really matter; the very revolution depended upon the continued existence of the army.

Congress had fled from Philadelphia to Baltimore handing virtually absolute power to Washington. He was like a monarch – George I of America. The army became the key to the survival of the rebellion. It was his lowest moment for the British controlled New York, New Jersey and Rhode Island. There was little enthusiasm for the war in Pennsylvania, Delaware and Maryland. Washington needed to do something to dispel the gathering despair.

The Hessian regiments had been given the task of holding the frontier posts and at his own request Colonel Rall, the hero of White Plains, asked whether he could have the command of Trenton confidently proclaiming, 'Those clod hoppers will not attack us'. Rall ignored a spy's report that Washington was preparing an attack for, like all the Hessians, they were expecting a quiet Christmas. One of his officers wrote in his diary, 'We have not slept a night in peace since we came to this place.'

Washington controlled all the boats on the River Delaware so he devised a daring plan to move most of his army across the river to capture Trenton. The troops under his direct control amounted to 2,400 and they crossed the river in ore barges in great secrecy on the dark night of 25 December through pack ice, a howling freezing wind, sleet and a hailstorm. Another column intended to cross the river to the south in a flanking movement but they never made it. The Hessians were taken by

The Grand Union Flag

This flag was raised at Washington's headquarters in Cambridge, Massachusetts on 1 January 1776. The flag carries both the Union Jack and the thirteen stripes of the thirteen colonies. The Declaration of Independence was six months away and the Americans in early 1776 were fighting for their rights under King George.

The Wise Men of Gotham and their Goose (opposite)
16 February 1776

Bute, quite unfairly as he had no influence at this time, slaughters the Golden Goose of America. The British Lion is asleep while a dog urinates on a map of America. Gotham, a village in Nottingham-shire, was for centuries proverbial for the folly of its inhabitants. The first collection of popular tales of stupidity appeared during the reign of Henry VIII and was called *Merrie Tales of the Mad Men of Gotham*. Some time in the 19th century New York was satirically called Gotham.

Engrav'd for the General Magazine.

THE STATE BLACKSMITHS
Forging fetters for the Americans
Published according to Act of Parliament 1st March 1776.

The State Blacksmiths – Forging fetters for the Americans
1 March 1776

Lords Mansfield and Sandwich are forging the fetters watched by a confident North, a steely Bute, and a fatuously smiling King George. In November 1775 North had brought in a bill to prohibit all intercourse with America and to approve the seizure of American shipping by the Royal Navy. This was war footing and the government made so much of petitions from some northern towns supporting the war that it stimulated retaliation by others who presented peace petitions. The war totally disrupted the extensive and profitable flow of trade across the Atlantic – in the early 1770s the 13 colonies took 20% of British exports and sent back 30% of British imports. This is just what riled so much of the City of London and a street ballad contained this verse:

> *Their ports and harbours, they've blocked up,*
> *And all their trade they stop,*
> *So all the poor are left to starve*
> *And we must shut up shop.*

The City traders led by the Mayor submitted a petition to the King asking him, 'to cast an eye on the general prosperity of this land and reflect what must be its fate when deprived of its American commerce.'

LA DESTRUCTION DE LA STATUE ROYALE A NOUVELLE YORCK.

Die Zerstorung der Koniglichen Bild
Saule zu Neu Yorck   La Destruction de la Statue royale
                            a Nouvelle Yorck

REPRESENTATION DU FEU TERRIBLE A NOUVELLE YORCK.

Representation du feu terrible à nouvelle Yorck, que les Américains ont allumé pendant la nuit du 19. septembre 1776, par lequel ont été brulés tous les Bâtimens du coté de l'Est, a droite de Barse, dans la rue de Broock jusqu'au collège du Roi et plus de 600. maisons avec l'Eglise de la S.te Trinité, la Chapelle Lutherienne, et l'école des pauvres.
Paris chez Basset Rue J. Jaquet au coin de la rue des Mathurins.

La Destruction de la Statue royale a Nouvelle Yorck
(opposite top)
1776

One of the consequences of George committing himself so openly to the support of his ministers in suppressing the American rebellion was that he put himself right in the front line, a perfect target for verbal critics and satirists. Junius had recognised in 1771 the importance of retaining royal dignity through distancing the monarch from his political ministers, 'Public honour is security. The feather that adorns the royal bird supports his flight. Strip him of his plumage, and you fix him to the earth.' By going into the forum himself George inevitably drew down upon himself the verbal lashing of the words of the Declaration of Independence on 4 July 1776. Five days later his gilded equestrian statue in New York was pulled down by people calling themselves 'Sons of Liberty'. It is interesting that in this French print the Native American Indians, as well as the colonists, are pulling at the ropes. An armaments factory at Lichfield, Connecticut, turned the statue into 42,088 bullets for American rifles. At the same time the name of the university – King's College – was changed to Columbia.

The Terrible Fire of New York (opposite bottom)
20th – 21st September 1776

The British had captured New York and Washington had retreated well to the north at Harlem Heights, when a fire started in a 'low grogery' called the Fighting Cocks at Whitehall Slip on the southern tip of New York. Fanned by wind from the south it spread rapidly up town destroying five hundred houses, about a quarter of the city. Howe told Lord Germain that 'The Yankees (New York loyalists) are convinced that the New England men set fire to the town'. The Governor William Tryon thought Washington had planned it but that was never proved. Washington reported to Congress, 'Providence, or some good honest fellow, has done more for us than we were disposed for ourselves.' This French print was in no doubt – Americans had started the fire and British troops were bayoneting suspected incendiaries to death.

surprise and had their own guns turned on them by a party which included the young James Monroe. Colonel Rall, who was playing cards while Washington was crossing the Delaware, tried to rally his troops but was mortally wounded. Faced with raking fire and men advancing with fixed bayonets, the Hessians surrendered after forty-five minutes. Twenty-one Hessians lay dead, 900 were captured, and only four Americans were wounded, including one future president, Lieutenant James Monroe. It was a daring, unexpected, brilliantly executed, totally successful raid. General Howe, ever-willing to shift the blame to some scapegoat, reported to Germain that, 'Rall's defeat has put us much out of the way. His misconduct is amazing, had he remained to defend the village he would not have been found.' After Trenton Washington had to appeal to the militia to stay on but there were no takers as their time expired on 31 December. In order to get them to serve just one more month he offered them a bounty without getting the approval of Congress.

Washington's comment to an officer who brought him the news of the Hessian surrender was entirely apt: 'Major Wilkinson, this is a glorious day for our country.' Just four days later Washington crossed the Delaware again and outflanked the British troops led by Cornwallis that were despatched to reclaim Trenton. Once again the element of surprise caught the British off-guard. Washington led his men on a night march to Princeton, eleven miles north of Trenton, and fooled Cornwallis by leaving his camp fires burning. At Princeton he put to flight the crack British 4th Brigade at the cost of 44 American dead. Howe reported a loss of 276 but Washington told Putnam that it was nearer 500.

He then marched further north to Morristown, a well chosen refuge for winter, as it could only be reached through deep narrow gorges, which could easily be defended. During the winter Washington's main concern was to hold his army together for so many were short-term soldiers, and his ambition was to instil a sense of discipline as strong as that of the British army, but he ruefully recognised that 'men who are born free, and subject to control, cannot be reduced to order in an instant'. He stayed in these winter quarters until 28 May 1778 and used this time to improve the equipment and training of his men.

In February 1777 when Lord George Germain at last heard of the disasters he gloomily commented, 'All our hopes were blasted by the unhappy affair at Trenton'. These two engagements were not set battles – they were daring raids which astonished the British and showed to all Americans that the game was not up.

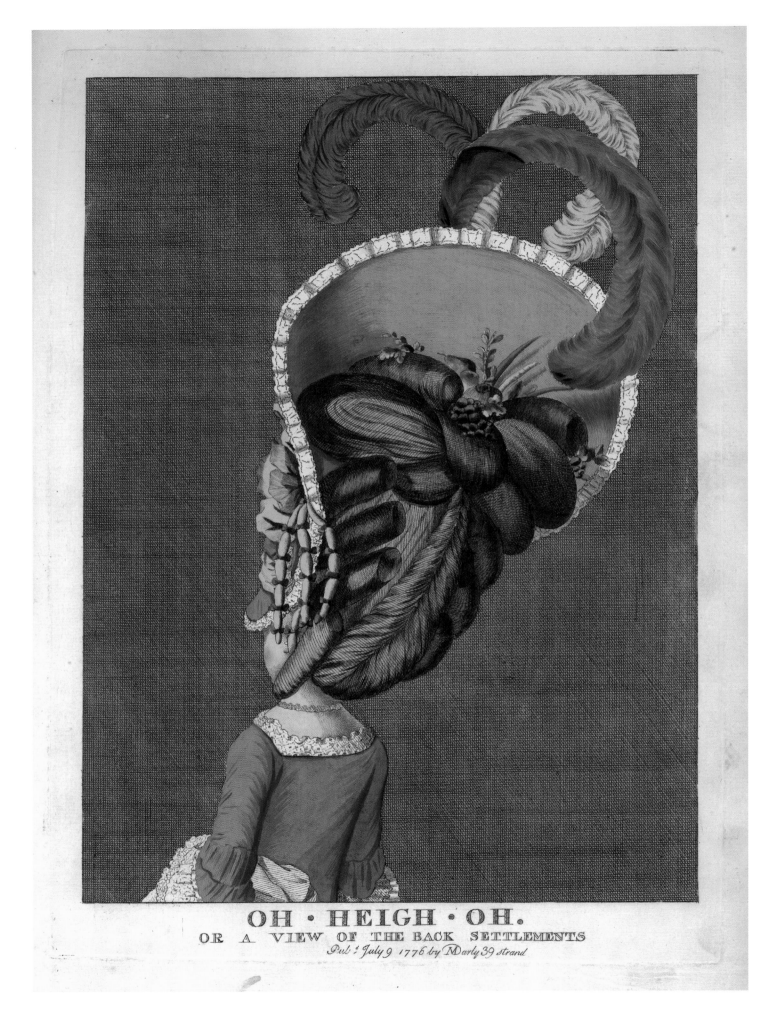

OH · HEIGH · OH.
OR A VIEW OF THE BACK SETTLEMENTS

Pub.ᵈ July 9 1776 by M Darly 39 Strand

Oh. Heigh.Oh – or a view of the Back Settlements (opposite)
9 July 1776
M Darly

This is a very rare print – it is not in the British Museum nor I believe in any American collection – and I am grateful to Andrew Edmunds, the eminent London print dealer, for drawing it to my attention. The Darlys had already used the fashionable elaborate hair decorations in their prints on Bunker Hill, Noddle Island and Carolina Sulivan. Londoners would have heard of Ohio as the Quebec Act of 1774 handed that part of America right down to the Mississipi to Canada, and it was called the New Quebec Territories. Thomas Jefferson had attacked this act claiming that the King 'had no rights to grant lands of himself'. The Darlys knew nothing of the land or its people and it is not meant to be representative – the closest they got to it perhaps is the apple, the pear, the grapes, and carrots – the great agricultural wealth of America beyond the Proclamation Line.

I am a Patriot
22 October 1776

The American patriot is presented as an irritable buffoon – he doesn't have to have a reason he simply hates anything that is done by anybody, even if it is to help him. His wife tries to cool his ardour; a dog urinates in his shoe, and one of his sons asks him to provide 'a Calf's Head for Dinner, for I'm sure the Patriots won't'. This rare attempt to belittle the rebels fails to recognise that they had good reasons to rebel. British opinion had underestimated the commitment of the American settlers.

News from America, or the Patriots in the Dumps.

Cornwallis invades New Jersey
20 November 1776

Britain was on the up. On 16 November British and Hessian troops overran Fort Washington on Long Island, the last outpost in the battle for New York and 2,837 Americans were taken prisoner. Washington was across the Hudson in New Jersey and Cornwallis decided to pursue him. In this drawing, thought to be by Lord Rawdon, British redcoats are crossing the Hudson in flat boats and then climbing, some manhandling guns, to the summit of the New Jersey palisades from which they marched against Fort Lee, only to find it had been abandoned. This was a brilliant manoeuvre that was carried out in the dark, not in the day as in this sketch. The Americans were in full flight over the Hackensack River further into New Jersey.

News from America, or the Patriots in the Dumps (left)
November 1776

In October the news of Howe's success in capturing New York reached London. At last North and Mansfield had something to cheer about, and Sandwich and Germain in the foreground gesture contemptuously at the English friends of America led by Wilkes. But the text in the *London Magazine* makes it clear that this was a false story: 'a fallacious and temporary success, the beginning of sorrows'. There were many in England who wanted the British to fail. Fox described the victory as 'terrible news'.

TO. TRENTON

HEAD QUARTER'S.

Head Quarters
1777

This is an anti-recruiting print. A recruiting poster on the signpost – in the shape of a gibbet – says that all gentlemen volunteers should report to 'three flying shit pots'. A recruiting soldier beats a drum on the bustle of a lady facing away from Trenton. In the headquarters there is another drummer, and someone is emptying a chamber pot on a soldier. Death in the shape of a noose is present. The message is clear – don't sign up for this dismal war.

The Battle of Princeton
3 January 1777
William Mercer

This is a contemporary painting by the son of the hero of the battle, Hugh Mercer. He was born in Aberdeen but left Scotland after he had witnessed the Battle of Culloden in 1745, where he saw the brutal slaughter of Scottish Highlanders by a British army. He became an apothecary but was soon picked out by Washington and promoted to be a brigadier general. He led the night march on Princeton and it was his brigade that was attacked by two British regiments. There was a fierce exchange of fire that checked his advance, but as he rallied his men his horse was shot from under him – the centre of this picture. Surrounded by redcoats he fought on with his sword, was repeatedly bayoneted, and left to die. Washington with the main body of the army quickly appeared upon the scene and rescued Mercer, though he died nine days later. In this painting Washington, with a flag bearing stars and no longer the Union Jack, went on to take Trenton and 300 British prisoners.

Chapter Five

The Yankees Triumph or Burgoyne Beat 1777

'Dreadful news indeed… an English army
of near 10,000 men laid down their arms and surrendered.'
Edward Gibbon

QUEBEC AUGUST 1775 TO JULY 1776 The first Continental Congress in October 1774 sought the friendship of Canada for they feared an invasion from the north. But the Congress also had the underlying ambition that one day Montreal, Quebec and Canada should be the 14th colony. On 10 May 1775 a group from Connecticut who wanted to take some land from New York led by Ethan Allen, a colourful adventurer, and his 'green mountain boys' seized Fort Ticonderoga on Lake Champlain, about 100 miles south of Montreal. He was joined there by Benedict Arnold, another adventurer from Rhode Island, who had planned to seize some British cannon. Both Allen and Arnold were later to defect to the British cause.

Congress, realising that the Governor General of Canada, Carleton, had sent most of his troops down to Boston to support General Howe, approved a further move towards Montreal and Quebec. This had the additional advantage in opening up another front which would give new heart to the rebels and the opportunity of acquiring more Native American land.

The American army was led by an Irishman, Richard Montgomery, who had served as a British officer in the Seven Years War fighting with Wolfe at Quebec. He captured Fort St. John just 25 miles south of Montreal and after a siege of two months he entered Montreal on 18 November 1775. Carleton, now appreciating the danger, made hasty preparations to defend Quebec. On 31 December Montgomery launched an attack upon Quebec assisted by Benedict Arnold, who had joined him after a foolhardy overland march from Maine. They breached the wall but by that time Montgomery had been killed by cannon fire, Benedict Arnold had been wounded in the leg and he realised that his small force was surrounded in a hostile city. It proved to be disastrous for 400 Americans were taken prisoner.

The British were helped by two factors. The first was the icy winter and the second was the outbreak of smallpox in the American army. On 1 May 1776 just before the Americans decided to withdraw over 900 of the 1900 American troops were ill with smallpox. The disease had also taken hold in Boston earlier in the year following the evacuation of the British in March.

The disease reached epidemic proportions and reduced the army's capacity to fight. On the retreat through the snow the healthy and sick were thrown together. Captain Lemuel Roberts, later recorded, 'my pox had become so sore and troublesome that my clothes stuck fast to my body, especially to my feet, and became a severe trouble to fortitude to bear my disorder.' The newly appointed American general, John Thomas, assumed his command on 1 May but was dead by 1 June. Mass graves had to be dug near Lake Champlain and in those few months about a thousand soldiers died.

Smallpox is caused by a virus and spread by human contact. An epidemic swept America between 1775–1782 affecting principally the American army and Native American Indians. The treatment was to isolate the victims or to inoculate them with a dose of the disease – John Adams was treated in this way and luckily survived. George Washington contracted smallpox in Barbados in 1751 but the attack was mild, and it left only a few slight scars on his nose. It was not until 1796 that Jenner hit upon the idea of vaccinating people with the much milder cowpox which produced immunity to smallpox. This disease has now been eliminated from the world – the last outbreak in England was in 1978. Washington called smallpox the 'most dangerous enemy' and in 1777 ordered his then professional army to be inoculated. Howe had insisted upon inoculation for his troops in 1774.

Small Pox Among American Natives (above)

American Native Indians seemed to be particularly susceptible to small pox. Missionaries in North America recorded that in 1781 a fur trader estimated that an epidemic 'carried off nine-tenths' of the Chipewyan Indians, north west of Hudson Bay. In an outbreak in Sandusky, Ohio in 1787 four out of six Native Indians died. In the Pontiac revolt of 1763 the British tried to spread the disease among their enemies.

This Native Indian record of an outbreak in 1780-1781 marks the spots on the face and neck of a Dakota Indian – indicated by the arrangement of the hair.

Small pox and disease did not hit only the Indians. In almost every engagement a fifth of the British force was unable to fight through illness. In the swamps of the South, the American militia had the advantage of an in-bred immunity denied to the British. Unhygienic camps, poor food, putrid fevers, dysentery, sunstroke and primitive medical services brought down more men than American bullets and bayonets.

The Siege of Quebec
January-May 1776

The rebel American army led by Montgomery and Arnold amounted to 1,000 men – the defenders of Quebec had 2,000. Montgomery attacked from the west alongside the St Lawrence River and breached the walls, but he was killed. Benedict Arnold attacked the Lower Town from the North, and was met by devastating cannon fire. Many were trapped in the houses of the Lower Town. Arnold was wounded and the rebels retreated realising that the expected support from the French Catholics had not materialised. Three hundred and eighty-nine rebels were captured; the rest retreated and began the long siege of Quebec which lasted for five months. The rebels made the mistake of relying upon a supply line that stretched back over 200 miles to New York State – a similar mistake was made by the British when General Bourgogne had to depend on the same supplies going in the reverse direction. In May the rebels realised that the siege was hopeless: they retreated and were relentlessly pursued by Carleton.

This print of the siege was made on linen and is the only contemporary engraving of this whole campaign.

THE NORTHERN CAMPAIGNS, 1777

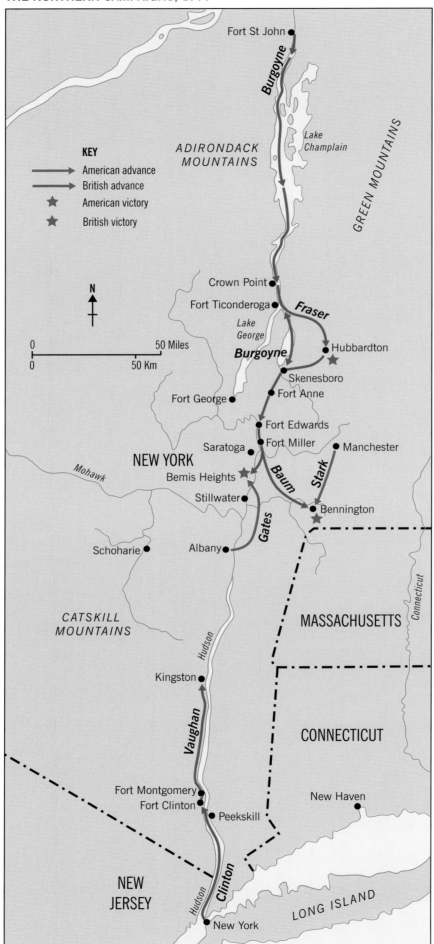

Fort St John

Burgoyne

ADIRONDACK
MOUNTAINS

*Lake
Champlain*

GREEN MOUNTAINS

KEY

American advance

British advance

★ American victory

★ British victory

N

Crown Point

Fort Ticonderoga

Fraser

*Lake
George*

Hubbardton ★

Burgoyne

0   50 Miles

0   50 Km

Skenesboro

Fort Anne

Fort George

Fort Edwards

Saratoga   Fort Miller   Manchester

NEW YORK

Mohawk

Bemis Heights ★   *Baum*   *Stark*

Stillwater   Bennington ★

Schoharie   Albany   *Gates*

Connecticut

CATSKILL
MOUNTAINS

MASSACHUSETTS

Hudson

Kingston

Vaughan

CONNECTICUT

Fort Montgomery

Fort Clinton   New Haven

Peekskill

**NEW
JERSEY**

Hudson   *Clinton*

New York   LONG ISLAND

Saratoga 1776-1777

Carleton's routing of the American army that had laid siege to Quebec for five months was one of the great British successes. Having destroyed the American fleet on Lake Champlain, Carleton withdrew to winter quarters in Canada. Back in London Burgoyne persuaded Germain to support his plans to lead an army from Canada, not under Carleton's command as Germain did not like him, south to Albany in New York State where he would join up with Howe.

The main aim was to drive a wedge between the northern and southern colonies, but this was a flawed strategy as any line of demarcation would need, as Alexander Hamilton pointed out in April 1777, 'a chain of forts and such a number of men at each as would never be practicable or maintainable but to an immense army.' Howe, on the other hand, had told London that his main strategy for 1777 was to occupy Philadelphia, the capital of the American rebellion: his earlier plan to send a force to Albany was quietly shelved. Germain failed to let Howe know of the plan which he and Burgoyne were 'cooking-up' and which led, amongst other things, to Carleton's resignation.

Burgoyne was a flamboyant adventurer – Walpole dubbed him, 'General Swagger'. There was a celebrated elopement with the daughter of Lord Derby; able and bold leadership against invading Spanish forces in Portugal in 1762; an election to parliament where he remorselessly attacked Robert Clive – an infinitely better and more successful soldier – a friend of David Garrick and a successful playwright; with a reputation as a rake and a gambler – Gentleman Johnny. He was so confident of the success of the British army in America that he wagered Charles James Fox a pony that he would be home 'victorious from America by Christmas 1777' – this wager was recorded in the betting book at Brooks' Club. Fox prophesised the result exactly: 'Be not over-sanguine. I believe that when you return to England you will be a prisoner on parole.'

All the ingredients of failure were present from the start:

The Cedars
1776

In the American invasion of Canada, a small American post was taken by British and Canadian soldiers together with some Mohawks. However, some British prisoners were taken and Carleton was alleged to have said, 'I have conversed with those who saw the scalps warm from the heads of our countrymen…and who beheld the fires lighted up, and heard the horrid shrieks and gloomy howlings of the savage tribes.' This may however have been apocryphal since the American general, Arnold, rode out to Montreal to attack the captors and to prevent the Indians murdering their prisoners. It was reported that he had arranged an exchange. Nonetheless, the author of this print wanted to bring home to his audience in London that Britain had launched a war that was savagely brutal.

Howe ignored the northern army; Germain did not inform Howe that it was a settled decision to march south; Burgoyne did not seek Howe's support; and Clinton did not tell Howe of the dangers of the Canadian strategy of which he was aware. Both Howe and Burgoyne wanted to administer the 'knock-out' blow. So pride, ambition, jealously, vanity and over-confidence ensured a fiasco. Moreover Howe had decided that the capture of Philadelphia, the seat of Congress, would break the rebels' will to fight – a catastrophic misjudgement which also meant that he had to abandon the loyalists in New Jersey who had stood behind the British for six months – the first great betrayal.

In July Howe, instead of marching across New Jersey to reach Philadelphia, decided to sail up the Delaware with 18,000 men in 260 boats, but on seeing the American encampments on the bank he abandoned the plan to land and was committed to sail around the long 700-mile Delmarva Peninsula to Chesapeake Bay, a journey that took 47 days and during which he lost most of his horses. Washington then realised that the

Poor old England endeavouring to reclaim his wicked *american Children*.

And therefore is ENGLAND maimed & fores to go with a Staff.

Poor Old England Endeavouring to Reclaim her Wicked American Children

1 April 1777

Matthew Darly

This prescient print appeared only nine months after the first engagement at Bunker Hill. England is an angry, puzzled, old man with a wooden leg and a cat-o'-nine-tails while the Americans are young, confident, insolent and defiant. It was to take another four years for George and his ministers to realise that their task was impossible.

British could not mount an expedition to link up with Burgoyne in the north and he must therefore defend Philadelphia, forming up his army of 16,000 men across the Brandywine River. In the battle that followed Howe demonstrated his brilliance as a tactical field commander by totalling outmanoeuvring Washington, whose army only just managed to escape. He frankly admitted to Congress: 'We have been obliged to leave the enemy the masters of the field.' There were 200 dead; 500 wounded and 400 captured. The British suffered only 100 killed and 450 wounded. Howe found another excuse for his failure to crush Washington's army: 'The enemy's army escaped a total overthrow that must have been the consequence of one hour's more daylight.'

Cornwallis was dispatched to enter Philadelphia which he did on 20 September 1777 to be greeted by crowds of loyalists singing 'God save the King'. The British also came across a camp of rebel soldiers at Paoli and there they removed the flints of their muskets, moving to attack just with their bayonets. This was a brutal massacre of sleeping men where 300 Americans were killed and 100 were captured; the British lost only 18. Washington planned a daring counterstroke, hoping to repeat

The Conference between the Brothers HOW to get Rich.

Trenton at Germantown. Again he was repulsed savagely and decisively by the British. Many thought the end of the war was in sight.

In June 1777 Burgoyne assembled his army for the invasion – 7,000 men including two German brigades of Hessians and Brunswickers; 1,500 Canadians; 300 Native Indians; and a huge baggage train to serve the needs of 225 women and 500 children. The march south involved travelling by both land and boat, and the first 100 miles were quickly covered. The first target was Fort Ticonderoga which had been a staging post for both armies in the past and it was considered to be the 'Gibraltar of the North'. As the Americans had abandoned it, the fort was taken without any fighting and the significance was so exaggerated that when George III heard of it he danced with joy saying, 'I have beat them. Beaten all the Americans.'

The Americans were once again engaged in the art, which they had developed almost to perfection, of retreating. The next 28 miles to Fort St Edward were much more difficult as there were marshes, streams and dense forests, and the soldiers, many skilled woodsmen, felled trees in their path, destroyed bridges and razed crops. Burgoyne had not studied the terrain in much

The Conference between the Brothers How to get Rich
10 October 1777
General Sir William Howe, Commander-in-Chief of the army, and Lord Howe, Admiral in charge of the navy, sent no news back to London in September or October, leading Horace Walpole to condemn them: 'The nation from impatience of news, grew much dissatisfied and the Howes were infinitely abused and accused of thinking of nothing but their vast profits.' The cabbages in the carts were slang for items pilfered by tailors – to cabbage meant to pilfer. There was a deep suspicion that the generals were making a pile of money from the war and therefore are happy to take the devil's advice to 'Continue the War'.

The valid criticism should have been directed at the casual, slow, procrastinating way in which the war was being pursued. He had the company of Mrs Joshua Loring, the wife of his prison commissioner, and this earned him the wit's advice:

Awake, arouse, Sir Billy
There's forage on the plain
Ah, leave your little filly
And open the campaign.

PROVINCIAL GENERAL BUTTONS *Marching to* SARATOGA *with plunder*

Provincial General Buttons Marching to Saratoga with Plunder

John Kay

Colonel Campbell, a British officer, became an American prisoner in 1776 and he was confined in a very small cell with only a tiny hole in the wall. Through this he saw several American soldiers and he drew the sketch of one 'General Buttons' on his way to Saratoga. Released by an exchange of prisoners in 1778 Campbell sent this drawing home to a friend who gave it to John Kay to re-draw 'who heightened its unique grotesque appearance by the fancy of the caricaturist' in order to 'have a little wit at the expense of brother Jonathan'.

detail and it took a corporal, Roger Lamb, to record how difficult it was to reach Fort St Edward:

'The face of the country was so broken with creeks and marshes that there were no less than forty bridges to construct, one of which was over a morass two miles in extent.'

Burgoyne reached Fort St Edward on 31 July and it was then that he first became concerned about the supply chain that stretched back 185 miles to Canada; for he only had enough food for a month. He despatched a German foraging party of 550 men under the command of Lieutenant-Colonel Baum, who was so confident that he took the regimental band with him, to Bennington, a well-farmed area to the south. He was met by a rebel army of over 2,000 militiamen under the

Saratoga Camp

The Generals in America doing nothing, or worse than nothing.

charismatic leadership of Brigadier General John Stark, a man known for his hardness. He knew that the Germans were in a trap: 'There are redcoats and they're ours, or Molly Stark sleeps a widow tonight.' Some of the rebels wore white paper in their hats pretending to be loyalists in order to trick the Germans, and Stark with clever flanking movements overwhelmed and mercilessly slaughtered them as they were encumbered with their high boots and heavy military sabres which were most unsuitable for forest warfare. This was a devastating day for British forces: 900 men lost: 696 captured and about 200 killed.

Burgoyne stayed at Fort St Edward during the whole of a very hot August, watching the wheel of fortune turn against him: the country around him was entirely hostile; crops were burnt; farmers became snipers and in an incident that was to pass into American folklore, a Native Indian in his army scalped a young American loyalist, twenty-three-year-old Jane McCrea as she was trying to meet her lover, one of Burgoyne's officers. Burgoyne refused to execute the Native Indian, which turned out to be a fair decision, for when her body was dug up she had clearly died of gunshot wounds. The horror of this tragedy spread quickly across America and stimulated the recruitment of militiamen to the rebel cause. Another devastating blow was that the force under St Leger, which was marching south to the west of Burgoyne in order to sweep out the rebels in the Mohawk Valley, was checked at Stanwix and his Native Indian supporters deserted him. Burgoyne's troops were now down to 4,000 men as detachments had to be left at the various posts captured during the march. The American army now amounted to 16,000; a fact that none of Burgoyne's spies discovered.

The Political Raree Show: The Generals in America doing nothing or worse than nothing
October 1777

Chatham on hearing the news of the surrender at Saratoga, which reached London on 2 December, called the Americans 'Whigs in principle and heroes in conduct' whose affection had been lost 'by employing mercenary Germans to butcher them; by spiriting up savages in America to scalp them with a tomahawk.' In this print Burgoyne is kneeling down to surrender the British flag to the striped flag of America. The British general with empty bottles at his feet and lounging at a card table is Sir William Howe who had not moved his army north to help Burgoyne.

A diary was kept by Baroness von Riedesel, the wife of the German commander. It is full of fascinating detail and she reported towards the end of the campaign: 'Burgoyne spent half the nights in singing and drinking and amusing himself with the wife of a commissary, who was his mistress and who, as well as he, loved champagne.'

Albany was just 40 miles away and it was still Burgoyne's target. He learnt on 20 August that Howe was moving towards Pennsylvania and Clinton, indecisive and weak-hearted as usual, was unwilling to offer any immediate help from his troops in New York. He had an opportunity, therefore, to abort the campaign and to retreat, just what Washington would have done in that situation. Burgoyne knew that crossing the Hudson towards Saratoga was his Rubicon. He gambled and crossed it on 13 September to find the American frontline was just 10 miles away.

The Murder of Jane McCrea
1777

Jane McCrea, a loyalist, was twenty-three years old, beautiful, with long auburn hair and in love with a British officer in Burgoyne's army. She was captured by some Indians on her way to a rendezvous with her lover. She was murdered and scalped and became an icon for the rebels as a terrifying example of what Britain's allies, the Indians, could do. As with many icons there was another version. Her exhumed body revealed three gunshot wounds, possibly from stray gunfire, and her scalp was probably removed from her dead body to prove her death and claim a reward. Burgoyne refused to execute the chief suspect as he did not want the Indians to defect. However he did have serious misgivings about using the Indians in British campaigns – they were 'at best a necessary evil; their services to be overvalued, sometimes insignificant, often barbarous, always capricious'. On the right the village of Esopus is in flames following Clinton's advance north in October 1777; another British outrage.

The Death of General Sir Simon Fraser
7 October 1777

In September Fraser, Burgoyne's second-in-command, had recommended a withdrawal from the trap which was closing upon them. But Fraser was killed on the first day of the Battle of Bemis Heights. As he falls he says, 'How hard o Frazer is thy Lot'. The German soldier in flight says the devil will have his carcass and the Scottish soldier exclaims, 'Now my lads ken ye not this one Arnold is hard at our heels'. This recognises Benedict Arnold's role in the actual

fighting when he rode up to the frontline rallying the troops and getting his horse shot from under him. Fraser refused to withdraw and was shot in the stomach. Baroness von Riedesel recorded what happened next:

'About 3 o'clock in the afternoon instead of the guests who were to have dined with me they brought in poor General Fraser upon a litter. The dining-table, which had been prepared, was taken away and a bed for the general placed there instead. I sat in a corner trembling. The noise got louder and louder and I feared lest they should bring in my husband also. The general said to the surgeon, "Do not hide anything from me. Am I going to die?" The ball had gone through his bowels.'

The Surrender at Saratoga
17 October 1777

When the news of the humiliation at Saratoga reached London this print showed Burgoyne – Gentleman Johnny – leading his shackled soldiers dressed as a playboy and carrying his plays saying, 'I have led my Rag-o-Muffians where they have been Peppered.' This illustration was part of a much larger print.

John M'Alpine, a British farmer who hoped to settle in America and was sucked into helping the army as a civilian, shrewdly commented on this debacle: 'I had not too sanguine hopes of their procedure, surrounded by numerous enemies in one extensive, disaffected country, very little known to our adventurers, who had not the support they expected, nor the encouragement they were entitled to.'

While Burgoyne dallied in August, the rebels joined by the ever-enterprising Benedict Arnold – the most versatile and enthusiastic field commander in the entire war – who had led the rebels to check St Leger by giving the false impression that his force was much larger than it was. General Gates assumed command of the rebels after successfully displacing General Schuyler, who had led the successful retreat from Canada, and he had built strong defensive positions with palisades of logs on the Bemis Heights, a small hill which commanded the Hudson. On 29 September, through a freezing fog, Burgoyne attacked, but after a series of assaults no ground had been gained and the American line had not been broken. Fraser, his second in command, persuaded him not to launch another attack immediately and he had yet another opportunity to withdraw. The Native Indians had seen what was happening and simply disappeared into the woods. Burgoyne learnt that another relief column from the east had been checked and the rebels had taken the outskirts of Ticonderoga cutting off his escape route. On 7 October he made instead a suicidal move by despatching 1,500 men to penetrate the American left which was thought to

be their weakest point. They were soon surrounded and Fraser, leading a relief party, was killed. Once again it was Benedict Arnold who seized the opportunity and led a charge which turned the British line – one of his soldiers was to recall, 'He was our fighting general'. He was wounded again in the leg – the same leg that had been hit during the siege of Quebec – but it was his action that turned the tide.

The British army withdrew to Saratoga, exhausted, demoralised and drenched to the skin. On 12 October Burgoyne and his officers recognised that as they were totally surrounded and running out of food there was no point in going on. There was to be no final battle at Saratoga, simply a surrender.

The American commander, General Gates, whom Burgoyne had privately described as an 'old woman', demanded an unconditional surrender but Burgoyne persuaded him to accept an extraordinary deal whereby all his soldiers would be allowed to return to England on the understanding that they would never serve in America again. On 17 October 2,442 British soldiers, 2,198 Germans, led by Burgoyne in a

The Murder of Jane McCrea

The Death of General Sir Simon Fraser

The Surrender at Saratoga

The Battle of Germantown
4 October 1777

This picture by the Neapolitan painter, Della Gatta, is a near contemporary account of the battle which must have been explained to him some five years later. The Americans on the right, under the command of General Wayne, advance to the cry, 'Have at the bloodhounds! Revenge Wayne's affair'. This was going to be the payback for the Paoli Massacre. The redcoats retreated but some 120 men of the 40th Regiment under Colonel Musgrave took up posts in a large empty mansion, Chew House, and successfully resisted all attempts to take it. They refused to surrender since they knew their fate. The two flanks of the Americans pressed on but in the heavy fog and powder smoke the left wing, under General Greene and his subordinate General Stephen, lost their way and fired on Wayne's men – Stephen was later court-martialled for being drunk.

Washington made the strategic mistake of halting the advance and was diverted to attacking Chew House with additional infantry and guns. He failed and in the general confusion was forced to retreat leaving 1,023 officers and men killed or wounded – the British lost 521. This was a serious defeat which revealed Washington's poor tactical command of a battle. After Germantown Washington's Adjutant General, Pickering, and another of his generals, Conway, lost confidence in Washington as their commander-in-chief, disliking in particular the way in which he and Greene offloaded the blame to Stephen.

The Yanke's Triumph, or B------e Beat
17 October 1777

Horatio Gates, a poor field commander, was a political general who cultivated friends in Congress, particularly Sam Adams, and a year earlier he had intrigued against Washington. He had just got Congress to replace General Schuyler who had prevented the retreat from Canada turning into a rout, with himself. He had a great contempt for all things British, particularly the British aristocracy being the son of the housekeeper of the Duke of Bolton's mistress. He was surprisingly a godson of Horace Walpole, and thirty-two years earlier he had been a lieutenant in the redcoat army. It is interesting that in this cartoon the reply to Burgoyne's, 'What shall I say?' is 'Say hunger tames Lions'. It was the lack of supplies, especially food, which reduced the British army's willingness to fight. The first thing the Americans are doing here is to give soup to the soldiers.

The Takeing of Miss Mud I'Land (opposite)
15 November 1777

The rebels fortified Mud Island, which commanded the mouth of the Delaware between Red Bank Jersey and Fort Mifflin in Pennsylvania, with gun entrenchments and below-water detonators. The Hessians had been held off at the cost of the life of their commander, Colonel von Donop. Howe's engineers built artillery platforms and began to bombard the island on 10 November which destroyed all the defences; the route to Philadelphia by sea was open. Here a bare-breasted American belle-dame fires a pistol and more effectively a cannon, which blasts out from beneath her held-up skirts, hitting the British ships, the Iris and the Somerset. Only the topsails of Lord Howe's flagship, the Eagle, can be seen. This was small compensation for Burgoyne's surrender in October, and it re-enforced the folly of Howe's strategy that capturing Philadelphia was the prize – it turned out to be a booby.

THE TAKEING OF MISS MUD I'LAND. NOV. 1777

The Closet

1777

The Closet was the inner sanctum where the King's most important ministers met with him. The Devil is telling Bute what to say, 'Be Bloody, Bold, and Resolute', although by this time Bute had no influence upon affairs at all. Lord Mansfield, one of the hate figures in America, is reiterating his never to be forgotten quote, 'Kill them or they will Kill you'. Germain has instructions for Howe and Burgoyne, while the King asserts his defiance and determination, obstinate to the last. This is a meeting of the guilty men who are ruining their country.

'rich royal uniform' rode out to meet General Gates who he greeted with, 'The fortune of war, General Gates, has made me your prisoner'. They marched to Boston to await embarkation. Congress, however, prompted by Washington who wanted to give no favours to Gates, decided in January 1778 to suspend the agreement as they had twigged what a very one-sided deal it was. Burgoyne was allowed to return but his men were held as prisoners-of-war. Congress had behaved despicably – 4,000 men were now to become prisoners and if they had known that they may well have preferred to take their chance by fighting at Saratoga. The birth of America was accompanied by the shameful abrogation of a solemn treaty.

The soldiers soon coined the phrase to be 'Burgoyned' – which meant to be surrounded and captured, but his shame was short-lived. His old friend, Charles James Fox, quickly fixed the blame on Germain whom he condemned as an 'ill-omened and inauspicious character' for not ordering Howe to

march north. On his return to London Burgoyne was refused a court martial, an opportunity to vindicate himself. Surprisingly, when the government changed, he was made Commander-in-Chief in Ireland in 1782 where he fell in love with an Irish actress with whom he had four children. When he died in 1792 he was buried in Westminster Abbey – not a bad resting place for one of Britain's most incompetent, arrogant and vain generals.

Saratoga was the transforming event not just in the war but in the emergence of America as a nation. Up to Saratoga it had been a rebellion, a defiant but very chancy movement and to secure its great goal, the Declaration of Independence, a victory was needed. Lord North and George III should have realised that the sheer size of America meant that the British could gain a victory somewhere and some hundreds of miles away the Americans would gain a victory elsewhere, but no occupying army could ever be large enough to gain and consolidate a victory everywhere.

The only leading British figure who recognised that the war was unwinnable was General Howe who decided to resign as commander-in-chief and rest on his laurels – the victories of Brooklyn, Brandywine, and the capture of New York and Philadelphia. Nemesis was to catch up with him later as he was the one man who could have crushed the American army but failed to do so, and he spent much of the rest of his life trying to redeem his reputation.

The Flight of the Congress
20 November 1777

This is one of the few English prints to celebrate a British success – in this case Cornwallis' entry into Philadelphia. The city was the constitutional capital of the revolution – the Continental Congresses of 1774, 1775 and 1776 and the Declaration of Independence all took place in Philadelphia. Under threat Congress had moved earlier to Baltimore but had returned.

The roaring British lion is causing 'the wild beasts of America' to flee; Hancock, the President of the Congress, is a donkey; Washington an armadillo; Lee a wolf; John and Sam Adams are foxes wearing collars; Putnam is a wild boar; and Laurens a tiger. The owl is probably Franklin as he carries a paper with 'Louis Baboon a Paris'. Philadelphia was occupied by the British in September 1777 and when the news reached London there was a wave of euphoria, but that ended on 2 December when they learnt of the surrender at Saratoga. This is one of the few prints hostile to the Americans.

Chapter Six

The Germans and the French

THE GERMANS

'Mercenary sons of rapine and plunder'

IN FEBRUARY 1776, Lord North reported to the House of Commons that three treaties had been signed with German princes to provide troops for America. The Duke of Brunswick was to provide 4,300; the Landgrave of Hesse-Cassel 12,667; and the Count of Hanua 700. Other states joined in later – Waldeck and Anhalt-Zerbst, but offers from Bavaria and Württemberg were turned down. Catherine the Great of Russia said she could not send a single soldier and Frederick the Great was no help either. In all 30,000 Germans were to fight in the revolutionary wars: 12,000 of them never went back home, some were killed, some deserted, some settled. In November Parliament was asked to approve £336,932.1.6 and 3 farthings for the Hessians and £93,947.15.8 for the Brunswickers.

Lieutenant General Knyphausen (below)

Knyphausen, a sixty-year-old veteran, usually grim and silent, was known for his habit of buttering his bread with his thumb. He led a force of 3,997 Hessians and 370 Waldeckers who landed in New York in the autumn of 1776. Howe decided to give this new ally the honour of taking Fort Washington in November – the last rebel encampment in New York alongside the Hudson River. The rebels were encircled and outnumbered 4-to-1. The old general led his troops up the hills and secured the surrender of 3,000 American troops who laid down their arms before him. On 26 December it was Knyphausen's regiment, commanded by Colonel Rall, which was overwhelmed at Trenton.

Hessian Troops (above)

Hessian troops were first used in the battles to capture New York. In the Battle of Brooklyn they were in the centre of the line and, after the British under General Grant had opened the attack on the left, General Heister ordered the advance. To the sound of drums and trumpets they soon overran the American position as the American troops were terrified of the Germans: their general said, 'they surrendered immediately and begged on their knees for their lives.' In the battle General Grant reported fifty-nine British dead, 267 wounded; but Washington had lost between 700 and 1,000. Of the Hessians, only five were killed and twenty-six wounded.

The British had to pay the troops' wages but the princes were also handsomely rewarded: in one of Burke's apposite but wounding phrases they had 'sniffed the cadaverous taint of lucrative war'. The first contingent of some 4,000 Germans landed in New York in the autumn of 1776, and they looked ferociously magnificent: blue and white uniforms over yellow breeches; many blackened mustachios, and over their wigs coated with tallow and powdered with flour, the privates wore cocked hats and the fusiliers had tall brass helmets. They also spread terror into their enemy by singing as they advanced into battle; at Harlem Heights it was 'Nearer My God to Thee'.

They were immediately put to work in the Battle of Brooklyn where a British officer reported: 'We took care to tell

A HESSIAN GRENADEIR

A Hessian Grenadier
M Darly

The Hessians had won a reputation for plunder and this gallant soldier has a flask, a pouch, a leg of mutton, and what looks like a turkey in his personal baggage. The British soldier carried a pack weighing 60lbs – including a blanket, a water bottle, an axe, a musket and sixty rounds of ammunition. The Hessians out-did this – high jackboots, leather breeches, a sword weighing 12lbs, a heavy carbine, and some flour for making bread. Their helmets, swords and boots weighed about as much as a redcoat had to carry.

the Hessians that the rebels had resolved to give no quarter – to them in particular – which made them fight desperately and put all to death that fell into their hands…it was a fine sight to see with what alacrity they despatched the Rebels with the bayonets, after we surrounded them.'

Howe was pleased to have an ally and gave them the leading role in the taking of Fort Washington in November. There they established their reputation for seizing booty by stripping the rebels who had surrendered of their uniforms and clothes until they were stopped by a British general.

Stephen Kemble, a leading loyalist whose sister had married Gage and was then the adjutant-general, noted in his journal that the Hessians were 'Outrageously Licentious and Cruel to

such a degree as to threaten with death all such as dare obstruct them in their depredations.' Major MacKenzie, who served through the war, confided to his diary that the Hessians 'are not inspired by the high sense of national and personal honour which is characteristic of British troop'.

To the rebels the recruitment of foreign mercenaries was an unforgivable stain on British honour – they should fight their own battles. Chatham caught their feelings perfectly: 'mercenary sons of rapine and plunder. If I were an American as I am an Englishman, while there was a foreign troop in my country, I would never lay down my arms, never! Never! Never!'

THE FRENCH

*'As a French war appears to be inevitable
no more troops can be spared.'* Germain, May 1778

IN JULY 1776 the French Foreign Minister, the Comte de Vergennes, turned down an official American request for 200 cannon, 200,000lbs of powder and 25,000 men, but the consolation prize was that French ports would not be closed to ships taking supplies to America. There were many clandestine shipments and a small island in the Dutch West Indies, St Eustatius, was used as a staging post. Benjamin Franklin, who had then returned to France, had a personal interest in engaging French support since he received commission on goods supplied to America; an arrangement which Vergennes condoned.

DESTAING.

France was content to see its old enemy committing its resources to another war and Saratoga had showed the British were not invincible. There was a clear French interest in prolonging the war. 1777 was the last year when Britain fought only the Americans.

In February 1778 a treaty of amity and commerce was signed in which France pledged to support American independence, and by June France and Britain were at war. The French fleet, under the command of the Comte d'Estaing, arrived off New York and it was agreed that there would be a joint Franco-American attack on the British stronghold of Newport, Rhode Island. It turned into a fiasco. There was no coordination between the two allies which bred an early contempt of each for the other. D'Estaing was appalled at the poor quality of the American troops: 'All the tailors and apothecaries in the country must have been called out…

D'Estaing
24 February 1780
The trouble with D'Estaing was that he was a soldier – a lieutenant general – not a sailor. This print appeared after he had failed to prevent the British occupying Savannah. Like Rochambeau and de Grasse, he is depicted as an effeminate figure interested primarily in his exquisite uniform.

Marquis de Lafayette

Lafayette was a wealthy dilettante who sailed to America in 1777 to support the rebels and his first taste of warfare was at Brandywine where he was shot in the leg. In 1778 he met Washington and was promoted to a major-general to serve on the commander-in-chief's personal staff. He was useful as 'eyes and ears' though General Lee dismissed the handsome young men around Washington as 'earwigs'. Lafayette worshipped Washington who came to look upon him as his own son: 'I do not know a nobler, finer soul and I love him as my own son.' He became a trusted and competent army commander of American troops – the French were under the command of Rochambeau and he was actively involved in the Yorktown campaign.

In 1778 he was part of the disastrous French-American attack in Newport, Rhode Island where the Americans were so fed up with the level of support from the French fleet that a mob beat up some French sailors. Lafayette was insulted and he threatened a duel, peevishly complaining that he had 'been put in the position of hearing the name of France spoken without respect, and perhaps with disdain, by a band of Yankees from New England.'

they were mounted on bad nags and looked like a flock of ducks in cross belts.'

One of the problems was that few Americans spoke French and in some cases they had to revert to Latin to be understood. There were also tactical misunderstandings. D'Estaing set out from Rhode Island to try and find the British fleet and they circled each other, but no engagement took place as both suffered considerable losses in a great storm. D'Estaing then decided to move away to repair his ships. The American General Sullivan berated the French for deserting him, but under great pressure from the British troops he did manage to evacuate his men from the island. When searching for D'Estaing, Admiral Howe missed a great chance for cutting off the retreat: another lost opportunity. Clinton believed that if it had happened, 'the war in America would have finished, but the winds said "No".' It was no better in 1779 when the French were supposed to prevent the occupation of Savannah by the British, but failed to turn up on time.

France's entry turned the American conflict into a world war. Britain's attention was focussed upon the possibility of a French invasion and so troops that could have been sent to America were needed to man defences on the south coast. To Germain the need to protect the West Indies from depredations by either France or Spain meant that he ordered 5,000 troops to be sent from Philadelphia early in 1778. But this

so reduced the garrison in the town that Clinton had to abandon it; thus reversing Howe's great triumph a year earlier.

The battleground for the fleets was the West Indies. D'Estaing sailed south and occupied the tiny British islands of St Vincent and Grenada, but a more resourceful British fleet seized St Lucia. On the other side of the world, France received a devastating setback in India where Warren Hastings took the opportunity to occupy the French trading centres in Chandernagore, Pondicherry, Mahé and Karikal.

French help to America was to prove decisive for the presence of a French fleet off Yorktown in 1781 gave victory to Washington as it cut off any possibility of retreat by the British army. It was little wonder that George Washington danced for joy when he saw the sails of the fleet on the horizon.

However, being an ally of America was disastrous for France. It was an unnatural alliance between the monarchy of the ancien regime steeped in aristocratic privilege and a country in a state of open rebellion, sustained by republican sentiment, and ringing with the cries of 'liberty' and 'freedom'. Vergennes was not a farseeing statesman but a chancer who hoped to revenge the humiliation of the Seven Years War. He committed his country to a costly war from which they could gain little and which they could not afford. It helped to pave the way to the revolution of 1789 which saw the end of the monarchy and the aristocracy. What France lost, America gained.

Le Destin Molestant les Anglois

Destiny in the shape of D'Estaing brings a palm of peace to America while holding on a leash the dogs of war. All her goods – rice, indigo and especially tobacco – will in future go to France, Holland and Germany.

L'Anglais Corrigé comme un Enfant

The French cannot resist relishing Britain's humiliation. A Native American thrashes the bare bottom of George III while a Spaniard holds up his shirt, a Frenchman laughs and claps, and a Dutchman rejoices in the trading opportunities that lie ahead. The American War had become a World War.

COUNT DE ROCHAMBEAU
General of the Land Forces in America Reviewing the French Troops

Count de Rochambeau
1780

Lafayette had returned to France expecting to be the commander of the French army to be sent to America, but the veteran Count de Rochambeau was appointed and he landed at Newport in July 1780 with 5,500 men; less than the 8,000 men expected by the Americans.

This burlesque portrays the French as effeminate dandies: the commander-in-chief with a feathered hat and a long pigtail; and the men with large shirt frills, cuffs, and elegant shoes instead of boots.

Count de Grasse –
Taking a peep in the West Indies
Undated

This is the French admiral who made possible Washington's victory at Yorktown. His ships anchored in Chesapeake Bay prevented any English relief fleet coming to the aid of Cornwallis. On 2 September 1781, Cornwallis reported: 'Comte de Grasse's fleet is within the Capes of the Chesapeak [sic]. Forty boats with troops went up James river yesterday, and four ships lie at the entrance of the river.' He must have recognised that the trap was closing. When the news of de Grasse's arrival reached Washington on 5 September a Frenchman recorded, 'I have never seen a man so thoroughly and openly delighted'.

COUNT DE GRASSE
Taking a peep in the west Indies.
Sold by W.Humphrey. N.º 227 Strand.

Chapter Seven

1778 Impasse

'The want of Green forage does not yet permit me to take the field,
and their situation is too strong to hazard an attack with a prospect of success,
which might put an end to the rebellion.' General Howe, April 1778

BY THE END OF 1777 Washington had failed to save Philadelphia, and Gates – the hero of the day – had triumphed at Saratoga. A winter of intrigue and back-biting lay ahead with open plotting against Washington. Martha Washington had joined her husband and noted, 'The General is well, but much worn with fatigue and anxiety'. It was only in the spring when some officers made clear to Congress members that they would not serve under Gates that Washington's position became secure.

On 18 December his army took up winter quarters in the small village of Valley Forge – Washington would have preferred to have stayed in a larger town – and there they were to suffer the worst winter of the war. In the 19th century the myth was created that this was the time when Washington fashioned his 'New Army' as the brave patriots withstood a vicious winter with patriotic fervour. The reality was that the army barely survived the most appalling conditions. Many deserted as they were not paid and supplies ran out – potatoes, dough and unleavened bread replaced meat and one night the cry ran though the camp, 'No meat', 'No meat'. Local farmers were more willing to sell their crops to the redcoats who paid them ready cash. During the winter over 500 horses died of starvation.

Through incompetence, blankets and warm uniforms did not arrive and for weeks the men had to sleep in freezing conditions in tents, not huts. When Washington told Congress that he felt for his men who had 'to occupy a cold, bleak hill and sleep under frost and snow without clothes or blankets', they simply told him to plunder the countryside. The medical facilities in the early 18th century were primitive; in this case they were homicidal. In one regiment forty men were sent to hospital – in reality a charnel house – and only three survived. Howe's army, ensconced in the warmth and comfort of Philadelphia, was only twelve miles away and once again he passed up the chance of attacking, possibly obliterating, the demoralised and weak American army.

It was only when Washington's incompetent Quarter Master, General Mifflin, was replaced by General Nathanael Greene that the supply chain was improved. He was not a great field commander but his systematic and careful administration saved the army from disintegration. Morale started to improve and this was helped by the appearance of a self-styled lieutenant general, Baron von Steuben — one of Franklin's recommendations. He had served in the Prussian army as an aide to Frederick the Great, reaching the rank of captain — and he was not a baron either. He introduced proper drill, regular marching, and a common set of commands even though he could not speak English. He was larger than life; an ebullient bully, roaring obscenities, just like a regimental sergeant-major in the 20th century turning raw recruits into soldiers. The men who had been stuck in camp with very little to do for months on end welcomed the activity he created and by June 1778 the army was in better shape than the previous December.

In London the critics of the war harassed the government. There were censure motions in the House of Commons on Germain and Sandwich and throughout 1778 North had to use all his influence and patronage to secure majorities in the Commons and the Lords. The debates became more acrimonious and the parliamentary inquiries into the navy, the army and Saratoga were gladiatorial combats since Howe, Burgoyne and Keppel were all MPs who attended the House – the accused mingled with the accusers.

If North had had more confidence he would have sacked Germain and Sandwich but he did not have the mettle for that. At the beginning of the year he made the first of his many offers to resign, abruptly dismissed by King George III. In July he wrote to his royal master that the government needed a prime minister 'capable of leading, of discerning between opinions, of deciding quickly and confidently, and of connecting all the operations of government that the nation might act uniformly and with force. Lord North is not such a man.' George took this as a personal insult: 'No man has the right to talk of leaving me at this hour.' As this was not generally known at the time there has been much retrospective sympathy for North lashed to

10 Downing Street, but some of his contemporaries did not hold back. Burke compared him to Pericles in his decline when, 'Exhausted with misfortune, wasted with disease, and lingering with pain he walked abroad bedecked with amulets, charms and the saws of old women.'

What George and North failed to accept was that in several of the colonies royal authority had been overthrown. The royalist Governor of Virginia, Lord Dunmore, had abandoned Williamsburg, taking refuge on a British ship, while the Virginian Convention, with Thomas Jefferson and Patrick Henry, took over the government of that crucial colony. The royalist Governor of North Carolina had also taken refuge on a ship, as did the Governors of South Carolina and Georgia, while the Governor of New Hampshire had fled to Boston thinking it was safer. The British government's writ no longer ran and they failed to realise that America had become 'a nation in arms'.

A view in America in 1778 (opposite top)
1 August 1778
M Darly

This is a commentary on the American army at Valley Forge in the winter of 1777. The member of Congress, in a fur-lined coat and smoking a pipe, is well-protected from the cold, and seems indifferent to the plight of the army. The two officers seem rather proud of their troops and offer no sense of apology for their condition. Lying at their feet is a Negro who has been wounded, showing the disregard in which Negroes were held and the poor medical facilities available. The soldiers themselves are pictures of misery, ragged and depressed. This print must have been designed to improve morale in the British army.

A Picturesque View of the State of the Nation for
February 1778 (opposite bottom)
1 March 1778
Westminster Magazine

The cow is the commerce of Britain whose horns have been shorn off by America, while Holland milks her and France and Spain wait for their share. An Englishman wrings his hands in despair at the British lion sound asleep as it is being peed upon by a French pug. In the town of Philadelphia, a British ship is grounded and General Howe and Admiral Howe lie drunk or asleep.

After three years of war Britain had achieved so little that France, Spain and Holland are now poised to attack. This was the low point – North offered his resignation which was rejected by George III; there were repeated rumours of a major government reshuffle in which Sandwich and Germain would have been sacked, but they came to nothing; and three peace commissioners were dispatched to America on a fruitless mission. This print was so popular and apposite it was copied in America, France and Holland.

The Commsioners interview with Congress.

The Commsioners interview with Congress (above)
1 April 1778

The Peace Commission was headed by Lord Carlisle who was not even a minister and here is taking snuff, and consisted of the former Governor of Florida, Johnstone, who had fought a duel with Germain, and the minister responsible for the secret service, William Eden. It got off to a bad start as Johnstone had to resign following his attempt to bribe two members of Congress to accept the British terms. Germain, unknown to the commission, had ordered 5,000 troops to be sent from Philadelphia to the West Indies which meant the British had to evacuate Philadelphia where the Peace Commission was heading. They were miffed. They offered the repeal of all punitive acts, exemption from taxation, and the recognition of Congress, but they balked at accepting Independence – they wanted a political union. Congress ignored them and here they seem to be asserting their own terms. Their task was impossible since they had no authority to concede the very thing which would have ended the war, so after six months they returned to England in November 1778. This print anticipates the appointment of the commission which only set sail for America on 21 April.

The Commissioners (right)
1 April 1778
M Darly, from Darly's Comic Prints of Characters, Caricatures and Macaronies

This scathing satire appeared even before the commissioners had left England and it anticipates that the Howe brothers would join them – they are the first two kneeling – but they refused to act under Lord Carlisle. Each of those kneeling – Admiral Howe, General Howe, Lord Carlisle, and William Eden – spell out all the enormities to which America had been subjected: 'We have blocked up your ports, obstructed your trade'; 'We have ravaged your lands, burnt your towns'; 'We have profaned your places of Divine Worship'; 'We have ravaged, scalp'd and murder'd your People'; and at the end Governor Johnstone bluntly says that America can expect more of the same. The symbol of America bearing a cap of liberty glows with the success of her trade – she doesn't need to listen. What is extraordinary is that there were no prints that put the British case or derided the American rebels, even when the country was at war.

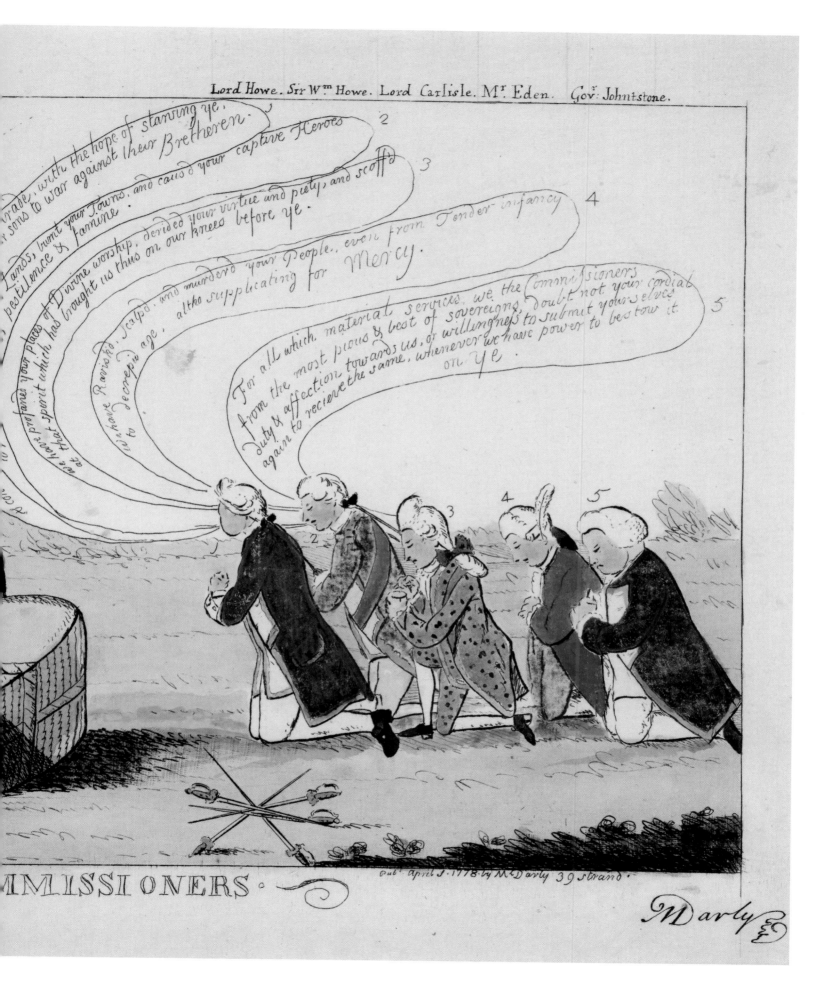

THE OLIVE REJEC.ᵀᴰ OR THE YANKEES REVENGE.

Pubᵈ as the act Directs may 4 1778.

LE LORD BURTHE COURONNÉ SUR UN ANE

Infortunéz Anglois, a quoi vos Bills Conciliatotre ont-ils servis?

1 Le representant de la Grande Bretagne pressé de fuir l'Amérique monté sur un Coursier a longues oreilles ne pouvant regagner l'Angleterre qu'a la nage, sa Flotte étant dispersé ou deffaite et ne pouvant lui donner du secour en ayant besoin elle meme par les Signaux de detreße qu'elle fait entendre de tous cotes. 2 plusieurs Americains faisant treve a leur moderation naturelle qui leurs enemis ont gratuitement qualifies de poltronerie, chaßent honteusement l'agent qui sous un voile honete voulait ebranler leur liberté en semant la division parmi eux. 3 un Anglois faisant partie du petite nombre de ceux qu'on souffre encor en Amerique tach de plus. . . vicaire l'animal. 4 un Francois representant son Pays digne soutien et allié du plus haut de l'Univers semprosse de couper le foible lien dont vainement l'anglois voudrait servir

The Olive Rejected or the Yankees Revenge
4 May 1778

This reflects on the failure of the peace negotiations. Lord North is wearing a crown supporting an olive branch which is falling off as he flees on an ass. He had proposed a Conciliatory Bill, shown in his pocket, to repeal all the punitive legislation of the past, but it was too late. Three Americans are chasing him away, angry at the 'poltronerie' of Governor Johnstone, one of the peace commissioners sent to America, who had tried to bribe two Congressmen. A Frenchman also assists by inserting a bellow into the ass and a sad Englishman, concerned about the anguish suffered by Americans, is trying to hold back the ass. This may well be a copy of a French print since all the commentary is written in French.

A strange air of unreality settled over the year 1778. In Philadelphia the British troops made the most of their rest and relaxation: balls, dinner parties, a German Faro bank in the City Tavern, and cock-fighting at Moore's Alley. To mark Howe's impending return to London a great party – The Mischianza – was held. For twelve hours there was a riot of drinking, dancing and feasting; a regatta with a military band on a barge; a huge firework display; and a midnight procession – the revellers were waited upon by 24 black slaves in national dress. When the news of this filtered back to London the headlines wrote themselves: 'Dancing at a funeral over the brink of a grave'. The London press also got news of the glamorous, colourful military adventurer, Cornet Bannstre-Tarleton, who had been caught in bed with the American wife of a senior officer. His defence was that he had butchered more men and lain with more women than anyone else in the British army.

Germain, reflecting on France's entry to the war, simply hoped that the Americans would come to their senses: 'We must hope that the rebels not having reaped that advantage from their

Dessine d'après nature, a Boston par Corbut, en 1778.   Gravé à Philadelphie par Sans souci.

DÉDIÉ AUX GÉNÉRAUX DE L'ARMÉE DE LA GRANDE-BRETAGNE PAR UN ZÉLATEUR DE LA LIBERTÉ

1. L'Ange de la France caractérisé par un bouclier chargé de 3 fleurs de Lys avec une tête de Méduse symbole de la terreur de ses armes. Il tient une épée flamboyante avec laquelle il chasse les Anglais 2 de Philadelphie. 3 Les Américains se réjouissent de voir renaître l'Age d'Or en Amérique, désigné par le Bonnet de la Liberté 4 avec leur enseigne attachée à un mât.

Anglais audacieux, L'Ange Exterminateur
Sauve Philadelphie de votre affreuse engeance;
Contre la trahison, la cruauté, l'horreur,

Il vient du juste ciel exercer la vengeance :
Vertueux Insurgens, voyez renaître encor
Avec la liberté, les jours de l'Age d'Or.

new allies which they were taught to expect, and our superiority at sea being restored, may incline many people to return to their allegiance and lie happy under the protection of Great Britain.' The King, too, added his own inspiration by deciding that 27 February should be a day of fasting and prayer putting more trust in the Almighty than in his ministers.

A year later the support of God was again sought by every vicar adding a prayer which started:

'O Blessed Lord…Do thou, we pray thee frustrate [the Americans'] wicked designs, defeat their stratagems, and put them to flight and confusion before his face, and grant that the success of [His Majesty's] arms, by thy blessing, may establish his lawful authority over his disobedient subjects…'

The sense of unreality also extended to the belief that it was possible to make peace with the Americans on British terms. Three commissioners were despatched to America to offer the repeal of all punitive measures, the foreswearing of future

The British retreat from Philadelphia June 1778

This French print is a piece of premature propaganda. The avenging angel of France/Medusa drives the British into a panicky flight while a group of Americans dance around a liberty pole. The French fleet under d'Estaing arrived in Philadelphia to find that the British had already left. They then sailed north where d'Estaing failed to give any effective support to the bungled American attempt to seize Newport and Rhode Island. So much for Medusa!

Monsieur sneaking Gallantly into Brest's sculking Hole after receiving a preliminary Salutation of British Jack Tar the 27 of July 1778

Publ: as the Act directs by W. Richardson N.º 68 High Holborn

Monsieur sneaking Gallantly into Brest's sculking Hole after receiving a preliminary Salutation of British Jack Tar the 27 of July 1778

August 1778

After years of neglect by Sandwich the British fleet could only count on thirty-three ships in home waters, whereas the French had a squadron at Toulon and twenty-five frigates and thirty men-of-war at Brest under D'Orvilliers. The British commander was Admiral Keppel, an opposition MP and scourge of Lord North. The two fleets met seventy miles off Ushant. It was inconclusive; both admirals thought they had won but for allowing the French fleet to regain Brest, Keppel was court-martialled. His Whig friends rallied to his defence and the charge was found to be 'malicious and ill-founded' – a hero once again. British prints, which never celebrated a British victory in America, found it much easier to castigate the French and glorify the British Tar – normal service had been resumed.

taxation, and even to accept American MPs to sit in Westminster, but – and here is the imperial rub – they were not allowed to recognise the independence of the colonies. After six months they returned with their hands as empty as when they had left.

The last great battle of the war in the north was fought at Monmouth Courthouse on 28 June 1778 and intensified the stalemate. Clinton, the new Commander-in-Chief, decided to abandon Philadelphia which meant securing the safe passage of thousands of loyalists who could not be left behind. Some left by sea, but the rest – an army of some 10,000 men and 1,500 wagons and artillery – marched north to the coast about eighty miles away to embark for New York. Clinton was a gloomy pessimist and this retreat could have been avoided if he had received more support from London, and if he had appreciated that the British fleet was stronger than the French fleet. The conduct of this embarrassing and humiliating retreat was painfully slow – the long column straggled over twelve miles and covered only thirty-five miles in six days.

Washington at Valley Forge realised that there was an opportunity to harass and even defeat the British army. He set off at a faster pace covering fifty-seven miles in five days. They caught up with Clinton's army on 28 June; a blisteringly hot day which was to lead to some men dying from sunstroke. At Monmouth Courthouse, Washington ordered General Lee and 5,000 men

YANKEE - DOODLE, or the
American SATAN.

The War at Sea
August 1778
London Magazine

After France had declared war the battle scene shifted to the sea. Britain had to fight a formidable navy with many recently built ships on three fronts: the American seaboard; the Caribbean; and the Channel in 1779. France even posed a threat of invasion and a panic swept the country. The British navy had suffered from Sandwich's long years of neglect and was fully extended. Here Neptune tries to console Britannia while scornfully pointing to the strange combination of a Gallic cock and the patriot holding the stars and stripes; but he's no real friend for in the background heavy storms scatter the fleet that had left England under Admiral Byron who had earned the soubriquet 'Foul Weather Jack Byron'.

Yankee Doodle or the American Satan
1778
Joseph Wright

This engraving by an American-born engraver is a counterblast to the populist view of the American rebels who were depicted as little short of savage barbarians. This young man is simply dressed, rather thoughtful and placid rather than war-like.

HANCOCK, and N—th, Suppos'd to meet.
And thus, *the first*, his thoughts repeat.
Let some, like Spaniels, own my plan.
In me, behold a different MAN.

1st North.

ATETE, á TETE
between
The PREMIER & Jno HANCOCK, esqr

J. Hancock, Gov. of
Massachusets
Oct. 1780,

Who eer'he'd call thy House his Home.
Wou'd with the mountain Tyger, roam.
Live on fine Roots, pluck'd from the Earth.
From whence Himself, like Thee, had Birth.

A, Tete, á Tete between the Premier and Jno Hancock esqr 1778

A long-haired John Hancock, the President of the American Congress, rejects the peace offering of Lord North. He tells the British prime minister that he would willingly live in the mountains with a puma and eat roots than recognise that Britain had the right to rule over his country. North, who is watched by a bust of the King and has a Pomeranian at his heels, points to his drawn sword. To emphasise the difference between the two nations, the trees in America are palms and in England they are leafy oaks.

to attack the rearguard of 2,000 men under the command of Cornwallis. These were confusing orders which put the American troops in a dangerously exposed position, so Lee sounded the retreat. When Washington saw Lee's army retreating to his own post he was furious, swearing at Lee and ordered them back. The British army, thinking they had the Americans on the run, charged against Washington's defensive positions on the hill – that was the British mistake. They slogged it out until six in the evening and then the British withdrew. It was a draw; casualties were about even, but the British had forty wounded men and officers who were too sick to move and so they were just left behind – a mortifying consequence of this war.

Washington realised that he had lost the best chance he ever had of destroying the British army. He had a volcanic temper which required strong self-control to hold in check but this lost opportunity made him furious; petulant and searching for a scapegoat, he settled on Lee for the predictable disgrace.

The Tea-Tax-Tempest, or the Anglo-American Revolution.
Orage causé par l'Impôt
sur le Thé en Amérique.

He was court-martialled, found guilty and dismissed. Lee's defence was that Washington's orders were imprecise; he was ordered to march into totally unknown terrain; and by withdrawing from an untenable position he had saved his men; but that did not wash with Washington. He accused Lee of 'misbehaviour before the enemy on the 28th instant, in not attacking them as you had been directed, and in making an unnecessary, disorderly and shameful retreat.' The saviour of America had saved himself again.

Clinton scrambled home to the coast and embarked just a week before the French fleet appeared that would have stopped him getting to the safety of New York. So, after three years of war, the British were in exactly the same position as at the start: they had secured a foothold in America in 1778 – New York – just as Boston had been in 1775. They were locked into a small enclave on the coast: no land had been taken; no imperial authority established; and they had nothing to show for it.

The Tea-Tax –Tempest, or the Anglo-American Revolution 1778
Carl Guttenberg of Nuremberg

Time is showing to four women representing America, Africa, Europe and Asia the calamity facing Britain in America. The tea tax and the stamped documents in the fire blow the lid off the tea pot while American troops under their flag advance as the British redcoats flee below a flag with three leopards that represents the royal standard. The whole world stands amazed that a tax on tea could lead to such a disaster.

This print sold well in Germany, Holland and France but in later versions sold in France the Gallic cock blowing the bellows was removed, presumably because France did not want formally to acknowledge that they had been helping the Americans behind the scenes. This popular print also appeared in an English version in 1783 in which a despairing Britannia replaced Europe.

AN *EXTRAORDINARY* Gazette *or the* DISAPOINTED POLITICIANS. Nº 6

An Extraordinary Gazette, or the Disappointed Politicians
August 1778

The coffee house habitués wait anxiously for good news from America, but there is none – one tears up a paper in disgust; another reads in *The Gazette* about the Battle of Monmouth Courthouse that occurred just before Clinton managed to escape back to New York, and which both sides claimed as a victory. One map of America on the wall shows the extent of the colonies when the Elder Pitt was prime minister in 1762; the other print is a shrunken fragment of the colonies' map covered by writhing serpents in 1778. The painting on the wall of *The Mountain in Labour* is an ironic comment on the vast military effort in America which had produced just a mouse.

General Charles Lee (left)

Lee was Washington's scapegoat for the failure at Monmouth Courthouse to wipe out the rearguard of Clinton's army on its march to the coast. Washington's orders were not clear and he condemned Lee without being a witness to the engagement from which Lee had to retreat. He was charged with disobeying an order, court-martialled and cashiered in 1780. He died two years later, heavily in debt, and lambasting Washington to the last: 'A puffed-up charlatan, extremely prodigal of other men's blood, and a great oeconomist of his own.'

Dessiné d'après nature à Boston par Corbut en 1778   , et gravé à Philadelphie par Vd de bon cœur

DEDIE AUX MILORDS DE L'AMIRAUTÉ ANGLAISE PAR UN MEMBRE DU CONGRÉS AMÉRICAIN

1 *Un Amiral attaché à un arbre, ayant aux pieds et aux mains des serres de Vautour et des ailes.* 2 *Le Congrès Américain lui coupe celles des pieds.* 3 *l'Espagnol tient une des ailes tandis qu'un* Français 4 *la lui coupe pour empecher son vol.* 5 *Un autre* Français *emporte des rouleaux de Tabac.* 6 *Un* Anglais *au désespoir casse ses pipes.* 7 *Un gros* Hollandais *s'enrichit des plumes qu'il arrache de l'autre aile du Vautour, tandis que son associé* 8 *fait le commerce à la barbe de l'Angleterre.*

Tel qu'un àpre Vautour devorant l'Amérique,   Mais pour la bien venger d'un traitement inique
Anglais, impunément tu crûs la mettre à sac: Il ne t'y reste pas une once de Tabac.

Dedie aux Milords de l'Amirauté Anglaise par un Membre du Congrés American

1778

Designed in Boston and engraved in Philadelphia

This French-inspired print seizes on the pending isolation of Britain and particularly the vulnerability of her fleet. France was already at war – here cutting off the wings from an English admiral and seizing rolls of American tobacco – while Spain, which was to declare war in 1779, helps the French, and Holland, who was to join in during 1780, plucks the feathers and steals the trade. America is given the rather modest role of cutting the admiral's talons. This was really a recognition that Britain was now engaged in a world war and many prints were to depict the three countries alongside an American Indian.

The Curious Zebra (next page)

3 September 1778

The zebra is America and its stripes bear the names of the thirteen colonies. George Grenville is loading a saddle – the Stamp Act; North is holding the halter, declaring, 'I hold the Reins and will never quit them till the Beast is Subdued'. The three in the background are commissioners sent to try to negotiate a peace settlement: Lord Carlisle, William Eden and Governor Johnstone, an ex-governor of West Florida, who in the Commons had opposed the war. Eden says, 'Our Offers are Rejected, no terms but Independence'.

The figure in red on the right is a Frenchman who says, 'You are doing un grand Sottise, and Beggar I will avail myself of it'. The one in blue is George Washington, who says (alluding to his famous tactic of delaying full-scale battles with the British), 'My name is Fabius the Second, & the Rudder is my Hand. Pull Devil, Pull Baker, but She'll Stand upon her legs at last.' It is interesting that the print-maker in London did not turn him into a figure of ridicule or hatred, which was the way that Napoleon was treated later.

A TRIP TO COCKS HEATH. *Pub. Oct. 28 1778 by W. Humphrey.*

The English and American Discovery
November 1778

This charming small print is one of the first to designate an American as 'Brother Jonathan'. He sits with an Englishman, possibly John Bull, in a friendly way drinking and smoking together, telling him, 'Brother, Brother, we are both in the wrong'. By the end of the year all the tentative approaches to end the war had run into the ground.

A Trip to Cocks Heath
28 October 1778
J Mortimer

Two ageing brothel-keepers are bringing their stable of whores to visit the part-time soldiers at Cox Heath, whose evident joy is seen in the rampant cannons. George III visited the camp on 3 November. Britain was prepared at least for something.

The Graces of Cox-Heath (opposite)
1778
Matthew Darly

As France threatened to invade England and voluntary militias were raised, Darly could not resist poking fun at the amateur soldiers preparing for battle in the camp at Cox Heath. Twenty-five years later, when Napoleon's army at Calais threatened England, no print like this appeared; the French were depicted as effeminate, weak and knock-kneed, and the British as dogged and as robust as John Bull. Perhaps in the 1770s deep down the British people simply could not concede that after victory in the Seven Years War a French army would best a British one. This print might not be so fanciful for George III did consider distributing pikes to 'the Country People'.

Pub Nov.r 5 1778 by Darly 39 Strand

THE GRACES of COX-HEATH

Chapter Eight

1779

'Are we not at the moment assured that Washington cannot possibly amass an army of above 8,000 men? And yet Clinton with 20,000 men and with the hearts, we are told, of three parts of the colonies, dares not show his teeth without the walls of New York!...We have bullied and threatened and bayed, and nothing will do.' Horace Walpole

NOTHING HAPPENED IN 1779 THAT furthered the cause of either America or Britain; it almost seemed as if the war was put on hold. From the American point-of-view there had been no strategic follow-up to Saratoga and the abandonment of Philadelphia by the British: the moral advantage that they had had ebbed away. France's entry into the war had been trumpeted, but the first Franco-American combined operation at Rhode Island had been a bungled fiasco that created bad blood between the two allies. France was much more interested in fighting Britain in the Caribbean or even planning an invasion of Britain than risking engagements along the American coast which offered neither prestige nor prizes. Washington was appalled that Congress bickered amongst themselves, failing to send him the resources in men, money and supplies that he desperately needed. He told a Virginian delegate to Congress: 'Friends and foes seem now to combine to pull down the goodly fabric we have hitherto been raising at the expense of so much time, blood and treasure.'

By 1779 Washington had adopted a policy of attrition – the attrition of the British will to win. The longer the war lasted, he reasoned, the will of the British government would erode, they would be diverted to other campaigns by France and Spain, and he hoped that Britain would come to realise that they would never be able to control the colonies in America. Therefore there was no need or any sense of urgency to bring the matter to a head. Apart from re-taking the small fort at Stony Point to the north of New York on the Hudson (it was later abandoned to the British), Washington took no significant military initiative in 1779.

In Britain the will to continue was reinforced by the King. He told North in January that he would refuse 'to accept Ministers with any doubts about the imperial mission', but there had been an important change in the war aim. After the commissioners had failed to secure reconciliation in 1778, Britain had to accept that it had exclusively to bring about the defeat and conquest of the colonies. Unlike Howe, Clinton did not have the dual role of soldier and diplomat – his task was to crush the American army. In the winter of 1778-79 that army was under strength and demoralised, but instead of attacking it he settled for a few marauding parties and the burning of some small towns on the coast: Portsmouth, Norfolk, Gosport and Suffolk.

Clinton was by nature very cautious and his concern not to be the fall guy for losing America reinforced his natural timidity. Germain – remote in London –urged him to take action, to which Clinton fairly responded that being the man on the spot only he could decide what action to take. Writing home to his friend, the Duke of Newcastle, Clinton said: 'to risk fortune, health, and even reputation upon events to which I cannot give the least bias is hard indeed.'

For the first five months of 1779 London was preoccupied by the two court martials of Augustus Keppel and then Hugh Palliser arising from the Battle of Ushant in July 1778. Keppel, a favourite of the Whigs and himself an MP, demanded a court martial to refute the allegations that he had let most of the French fleet escape – his enemies which included the Navy Secretary, Lord Sandwich, and his fellow officer, Palliser, were hoping for a guilty verdict and the same sentence of death that Admiral Byng had suffered in the Seven Years War. The newspapers and the prints held the attention of the politicians right up until the end of May which marked the end of the court martial of Palliser. It was amazing that raking over the circumstances of an inconclusive engagement which had taken place eight months earlier was at the heart of British politics. Added to that, there were the inquiries by the House of Commons into the military failures of Howe and Burgoyne, but as both of them were MPs they spoke endlessly in their defence. Shifting the blame was the major concern of the generals and the ministers, rather than the resolute commitment to victory.

The Birth-day Ode
4 June 1779

The poet laureate's duty was to provide an ode on the King's birthday – they were invariably banal, sycophantic and unmemorable. This ode is played by what were the War Cabinet if there had been one – North on the fiddle, Sandwich on the kettledrums and Germain on the flute. The verses accompanying this broadside end with a full chorus, which clearly pins the blame not on the King but on his servants:

Yes – we will our Schemes pursue,
We will the Wreath of Glory wear;
His Worth's the same in Joves' impartial Eyes,
Who saves a sinking Empire, or destroys.

An English Jack-Tar giving Monsieur a Drubbing (opposite)
1 May 1779

This is the return of normal service! In May the long saga of the court martials of Keppel and Palliser over the Battle of Ushant which had been fought on 27 July 1778, had finally come to an end. Keppel had claimed victory in the battle but a large number of French vessels had managed to seek refuge in Brest. This led to accusations from Palliser, supported by Sandwich, and Keppel demanded a court martial to clear his name. This print has no doubt about the outcome: the inn is named 'Admiral Keppel' and offers to true messmates 'Keppel's cordial'. His ship, *The Victory*, is in port and a sturdy British tar thrashes a dandified Frenchman while a British terrier mauls a French poodle. The media in London were more preoccupied with the fight against France than the skirmishing in America.

A View of Plymouth

A raree showman is exhibiting his peepshow to Lord Amherst who was the Lieutenant-General of the Ordinance and from March 1778 the Commander-in-Chief. On looking inside he will see, 'Cannons without Carriages & Carriages without Cannons. There you see Generals without Orders'. In a debate a week earlier Fox had denounced the defenceless state of Plymouth as having 'cannons with no balls'. Even the grenadier on the left is grinning. Amherst, the nominal Commander-in-Chief, had no influence over the generals in America which only emphasised the lack of essential central strategic planning.

Paul Jones shooting a sailor who had attempted to strike his colours in an engagement (opposite)
1779

Paul Jones, a Scottish slaver and pirate, stunned England by a handful of daring raids on English coastal towns with just one ship. This is an episode in the bloody three-hour battle between Jones' ship *The Serapis* and a British man-o-war when a gunner shouted for quarter and Jones knocked him down with the butt of his pistol. It added to the glorification of Jones who was given a golden medal by Congress.

The Present State of the Nation
1779
J Phillips

In June Holland joined in the war against Britain and this is an early appearance of a Dutchman picking John Bull's pocket. John Bull is asleep and so America grasps the cap of Liberty, but he is being saved by a tough Scotsman holding off a dandified French aristocrat. Clearly poor old England needed more Scots.

The Horse America, Throwing his Master
1 August 1779

The British army, bottled up in New York, was only capable of waging a defensive war and France, here depicted as a soldier carrying a fleur-de-lys flag, had sided with the American rebels. The print depicts the ultimate defeat of Britain and the guilty man thrown by the stallion of America is George. In 1779 George intervened regularly to bolster the lack of resolve of North, whose pleas to resign were promptly rejected. In June he wrote to his Prime Minister, 'I do not yet despair that with the activity Clinton is inclined to adopt and the Indians in the rear, that the provinces will even now submit.' His optimism and resolution was not matched by a rational assessment of the operational difficulties of the British armies in North America.

Prattle the Political Apotecary
12 August 1779
M Darly

This Pall Mall apothecary is an armchair expert on the war. The Prattles and the Fiddle Fuddles and their coffee house friends were full of advice on how to win the war: 'cut 'em off pass the Susquahamma and proceed to Boston'. They knew nothing of America and this was picked up from Lord Howe's defence of his conduct that led to the surrender at Saratoga.

The other concern was that the entry of France and Spain in 1779 and Holland in 1780 to the war had turned the conflict into a world war. The battle ground shifted to Gibraltar which Britain held and Dominica (1778), St Vincent and Grenada (1779) and Tobago (1789) which Britain lost to the French and Minorca to the Spaniards (1782). In 1779 England was even threatened by the invasion of a French army supported by a Spanish fleet. There was panic and reserve forces were raised across the country and summoned to a great rally at Warley camp. The Home Guard of 1778-79 was as much the butt of humour as "Dad's Army" was in the Second World War.

The invasion alarm was intensified by the extraordinary exploits of John Paul Jones who became one of the most unlikely celebrities of the war. He started life as John Paul, but when he fled from his home in Galloway he added Jones and led a picaresque life – court-martialled for having a man flogged to death, and then to avoid a murder charge in Tobago he fled to America where he soon acquired the captaincy of a privateer to pillage British merchant ships. He sailed his twenty-one gun sloop, *The Ranger*, to the Irish Sea where a raiding party landed at Whitehaven, spiked the coastal batteries, and burnt a collier. Then a lightning raid on Selkirk where he grabbed the earl's silver, but on meeting the formidable countess returned it, much to the chagrin of his crew.

These were like insect bites to Britain but as with insect bites they swelled and itched. In 1779 he got a larger vessel from France and sailed to the east coast of Scotland where he fought a battle with a British ship, *The Serapis* – they were locked

The European Diligence
5 October 1779
Young Edger

A Dutchman pushes a wheelbarrow of Britain's enemies over the prostrate body of Britannia whom a Frenchman has stabbed with a sword through her heart – he is encouraged by an American in a feathered headdress, 'My Good and Great Ally Strike Home'. The Dutch were quite happy to trade with America and their island in the Caribbean, St Eustatius, became a trading post and supply depot for food, weapons and ammunition. They are being resisted, hopefully, by a Russian soldier, 'My Mistress is determin'd to Chastise you', but this was wishful thinking for Catherine the Great in March 1780 issued a Declaration of Armed Neutrality.

together, firing into each other's vessels for two hours. The British vessel eventually surrendered not realising that Jones' ship was about to sink. Jones reached safety in France. These escapades embarrassed and shamed the government; the British lion had been caught off guard. In America it was described grandly as the Battle of Flamborough Head, but it was a two-vessel affair and John Paul Jones sailed a French ship with a French crew. After this he simply disappeared from the pages of history, serving in the Russian navy from which he had to flee after being accused of rape, and he died forgotten in Paris in 1790. But not completely, for in 1908 his remains were exhumed and re-buried in a magnificent crypt at the Annapolis Naval Academy; not bad for a Scottish slaver and pirate.

TO HIS EXCEL.ᵗ GEN.ᵗ.

This Plate is humbly Address'd

Oh WASH'GTON is there not some Chosen Curse
Some Hidden Thunder; in the Stores of Heav'n.

M.ʳ TRADE & Family or the State of ye NATION

WASHINGTON PAT·PAT.ᵉ.

by His Obedient Serv.ᵗ Tho.ˢ Tradeless

'Red with uncommon Wrath, to BLAST 'those MEN,
Who owe 'their Greatness to 'their Countrys RUIN ?

Mr Trade & Family or the State of ye Nation
December 1779

This is a bitter comment on the economic misery arising from the war. This family is reduced to begging and the father lays the blame on the King, 'I was once a Capital Dealer but thro Ye Obstinacy of ONE MAN and ye Villainy of Many More'. So while they have to beg the King engages in his favourite sport of hunting. The two owls sing out, 'Long Live Sultan – as long as he lives, We shall never want, Ruin'd Towns and Villages'. George, engulfed in the scandal of the Hastings Diamond of India, was often depicted wearing an Indian turban. There is a plea in the poem to Washington 'to BLAST those MEN/Who owe their Greatness to their Country's RUIN'. This is a plea for Britain to be defeated by 'Thomas Tradeless'.

BRITTANIAS RUIN,

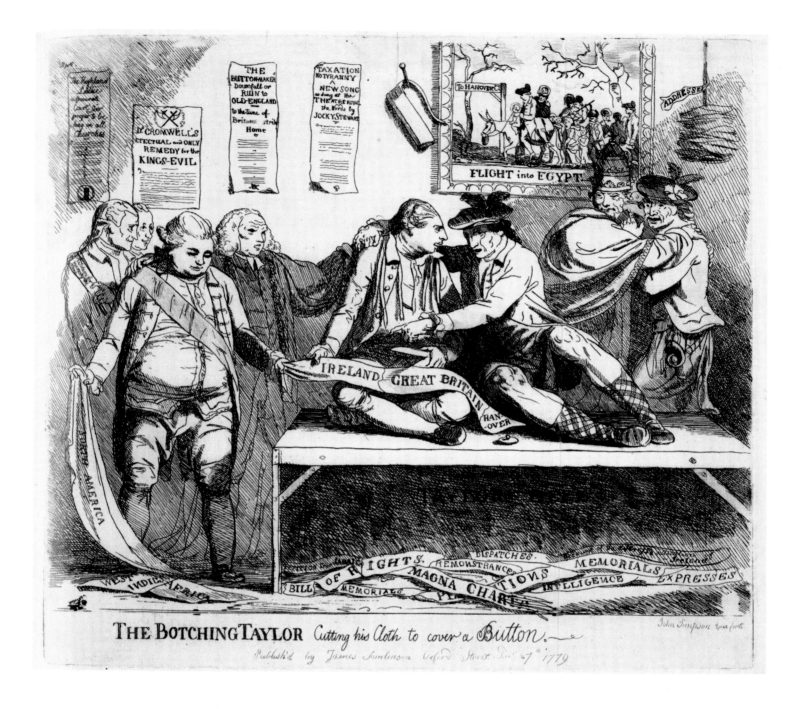

THE BOTCHING TAYLOR *Cutting his Cloth to cover a Button.*

Published by James Simpson Oxford Street Dec.r 27.th 1779

Brittannias Ruin (opposite)

17 December 1779

Mary Darly

Britannia, taunted by France, Spain and Holland, deplores her plight – 'Sold by an American, & purchased by France and Spain'. She asks for Pitt, the great leader and victor of the Seven Years War: there was no national leadership – it had all gone hideously wrong. Back in 1775 Pitt had warned that, 'foreign wars hanging over your heads by a slight and brittle thread: France and Spain watching your conduct and waiting for the maturity of your errors, with a vigilant eye to America and the temper of your colonies be they what they may be.'

The Botching Taylor Cutting his Cloth to Cover a Button

27 December 1779

John Simpson

1779-1780 was the low point for George III. The Whigs in Parliament attacked his extravagance and power; petitions from across the country supported them; and the news from America was dispiriting for virtually everyone now believed that Britain was engaged in a war that it could not win. George is depicted as the cross-legged tailor with little idea of what to do. Lord North holds the piece of cloth labelled 'America' which has already been cut off. The handbill on the wall refers to the ultra views of Dr Johnson – 'Taxation No Tyranny' – the cause of it all.

THE FRONTIER WAR AND THE
ETHNIC CLEANSING OF THE INDIANS

'Civilisation or death to all American savages.'

To the rebels the Native American Indian tribes were part of the enemy. In the lands that lay to the north of New York there was a series of vicious battles against the Shawnee in Ohio and Iroquois in Pennsylvania. The British supplied the tribes with rum and told their chiefs the palpable truth that the rebels were only interested in their land. In January 1778, 300 frontiersmen were wiped out in the Wyoming Valley by a great force of Iroquois and loyalists, led by Colonel John Butler. Then an extraordinary figure emerged, a Mohawk Chief, Joseph Brant, who had been hawked around London by Boswell to show off to British society. He linked up with Butler and they rallied their forces to fight off the rebel army, a part of Washington's army.

In 1779 Washington gave Sullivan the command of a force of 4,000 men to ethnically cleanse New Jersey and Pennsylvania of all the Iroquois. The orders were quite explicit: 'total destruction and devastation of their settlements' and 'the capture of as many prisoners of every age and sex as possible' for hostages. Sullivan's army boasted they had destroyed over forty townships and their winning ways involved torture, rape, and agonisingly slow deaths. Their weapons were bayonets and scalping knives. On Independence Day 1779 he and his men drank to the Toast, 'Civilisation or death to all American savages'. The grandiloquent words of the Declaration of Independence – 'certain inalienable rights; that among these are life, liberty and the pursuit of happiness' – did not extend to the Indian tribes and natives.

The area that was to become Indiana and Ohio became a battleground for voracious land-settlers. Virginia mounted an expedition under the twenty-five-year-old George Rogers Clark to seize as much land as they could and if possible to plant the Virginia flag on the Mississippi. They were met by another marauding party from Lake Erie under the command of Henry Hamilton who had offered bounties for Indian scalps. He was dubbed by that master of propaganda, Franklin, as the 'Hair-Buyer'; but Clark was even worse – he told his men that: 'to exceed them in barbarity was, and is, the only way to make war upon Indians and gain a name among them.' The bloody skirmishes went on through 1780, 1781 and 1782.

The British did not take the lead in the battles leaving it to the loyalists and to the Indian tribes as their methods of fighting were totally different and their allegiances were very fluid. There were many other armies at work: loyalists fighting for their property; Washington's Continental Army seizing land wherever they went; gangs of militias; and dispossessed German farmers and French settlers. Washington's Continental Army was engaged not only in ethnic cleansing but pitched in a civil war against the loyalists and, as in all civil wars, the cruelty, barbarity, savagery and hatred was intense on both sides.

Chatham in London thundered against the policy of using Germans and Indians: 'We had swept every corner of Germany for men; we had searched the darkness wilds of America for the scalping knife. But peace…would never be effected as long as the German bayonet and the Indian scalping knife were threatened to be buried in the bowels of our American brethren.' John Wilkes too lashed this policy, 'Merciful Heaven! Thousands of Indian savages let loose, by the command of a British general against our brothers in America.'

Indian Medal (above)

This medal depicting an Indian and a Britain smoking the pipe of peace was given to Indian chiefs for their support in the war.

Captain Joseph Brant (opposite)

This likeness was taken by the American portrait painter, Charles Wilson Peale, from life in 1797. As a teenager working with the British in the Seven Years War this Indian Chief took his first scalp at the age of fourteen. He fought alongside the British troops throughout the Revolutionary War being particularly effective in the raids and ambushes, which were notable for their savagery and cruelty, to the north and west of New York in 1779. The British found the Indian tribes difficult to organise and act collectively, but Washington had to divert quite large armies to prevent their revolt gaining more ground. After the war George III recognised their help by granting the Iroquois, the collective name for the Indian tribes, lands in Canada where Brant was to die. He translated the New Testament and the Prayer Book into his native tongue and he was for a short time a feted celebrity on his visit to London in 1776.

THE ALLIES.— *Par nobile Fratrum!*

Captain Joseph Brant – Thayendanegea (1742-1807)
– Chief of the Mohawks

The Allies – *Par nobile Fratrum*!
3 February 1780

In the Declaration of Independence, the King was accused of 'having endeavoured to bring on the inhabitants of our frontiers the merciless Indian savages'. Franklin, no less, forged letters implying that British officers had encouraged Indians to scalp the colonists for monetary rewards offered by George. With three Indians he devours the remains of a baby – there is nothing more vicious and amoral than the cannibalisation of the young. The whole world is turned upside-down like the Bible, and in the flag 'Grace of God' and 'Defender of the Faith' are half-obscured. A bishop leads on a man delivering scalping knives, crucifixes, and tomahawks. Of all the satires this is the most personal attack upon George III. There is a deeper meaning, for Britain was often described as the Mother Country and the colonists as her rebellious children, so the charge against George is that he is devouring his own young. This print also blames the King as the prime mover of the whole British policy towards America.

bravery aw'd they'll in a dreadful fright
nk back for refuge to the woods in flight
r British leaders then will quickly shake
l for those wrongs shall restitution make

A Scene on the Frontiers as Practised by the Humane British and their Worthy Allies!

This print was published in 1838 and it was meant to depict the actions of the British in the war of 1812-1813, but it also represents their activities in the Northern Frontier territories in 1778-1781. It accuses the British of using American Native Indians to kill and scalp patriotic Americans. It is a travesty of the savage marauding raids in the frontier lands where American settlers, encouraged by Congress and Washington, set about killing the Indians, raping their women, burning their houses, and destroying their crops. The price for a male scalp in South Carolina was £75, and in Pennsylvania $1,000. In Kentucky militiamen invaded Shawnee villages and dug-up graves to scalp the corpses, and a dead Indian prisoner was worth more than a live one. From 1775 to 1783 the scorched earth policy was ruthlessly and mercilessly followed. There was deliberate ethnic cleansing in Cherokee country where the men of William Henry Drayton were told to, 'Cut up every Indian Cornfield and burn every Indian Town'. So much for the grandiose words of the Declaration of Independence. It was the most shameful and disgraceful part of the Revolutionary War.

ENDGAME: THE NORTH

The skirmishing in the area north of New York was the scene in 1780 of two dramatic events involving two of the most colourful figures of the war. The British were firmly entrenched in New York, but in July 1779 there had been a successful rebel raid on a British fort a few miles to the north on the Hudson River – it was abandoned within days by the Americans. This led Clinton to set his mind on capturing West Point, an almost impregnable garrison of American rebels, a further fifteen miles to the north which Washington called 'the key to America'. West Point was under the command of one of the most charismatic American generals, Benedict Arnold. He was the best army commander on the American side, but having been overlooked by Congress, he had decided by the summer of 1780 to desert the rebel cause. On 25 September 1780, Washington arrived at West Point only to find no official welcome for the commander-in-chief and no Arnold. He was soon to discover the reason for on the previous evening Major John André, Adjutant-General to the British army, had been captured by three rebels and the papers he carried revealed that Arnold and André had met to plan a British attack on West Point which would be poorly defended. Capturing the garrison would have destroyed an important base, making the town of Albany indefensible, and may well have broken the American army's spirit which was at low ebb.

André, disobeying instructions, had worn civilian clothes for his meeting with Arnold. This gave the Americans the opportunity to charge him as a spy. Washington was ruthless and within days an extraordinary court martial was set up which consisted of fourteen generals, including Lafayette and von Steuben, and presided over by Nathanael Greene. Justice was collective but swift for the court sat for just one day. On his conviction, Washington insisted that he should be hanged as a common felon. Washington was shocked and appalled at Arnold's defection and as André had been the agent of betrayal, he was not going to be let off. André's execution was not only a warning but also a surrogate act of revenge. Washington did not stay to watch the execution at which André faced death with brave serenity, which won the respect of his captors. He placed his own handkerchief around his eyes and before the trap sprang he declared: 'I pray you bear witness that I meet my fate like a brave man.' At last a British hero had emerged from the war and George III granted a pension to his mother, a knighthood to his brother, and a memorial in Poets Corner in Westminster Abbey.

The Unfortunate Death of Major John André, Adjutant General to the English Army at Head Quarters in New York, October 2nd 1780 who was found in the American Lines in the character of a Spy
1780

André had been planning for over two years the defection of America's most talented general, Benedict Arnold. In 1778 André had been Howe's spymaster in Philadelphia where he flirted with a very pretty Peggy Shippen. Arnold, turned down for promotion by Congress, was given the governorship of Philadelphia after the British left. He fell in love with Peggy and married her. Arnold corresponded with André in code using invisible ink in letters sent by Peggy to a friend. Arnold promised to surrender West Point to the British, but the plans were discovered after a clandestine meeting. Washington rejected Clinton's attempt to save André, and insisted that he should be hanged as a spy, rather than shot as an officer.

The Loss of Eden – and Eden! Lost

This print was published later when Sir William Eden – he of the Conciliation Commission – was bought-off with a job by William Pitt. As a traitor he is welcomed by the famous American traitor, Benedict Arnold, depicted in the regimental uniform of a British officer. Arnold had gained his liberty but lost his reputation. He was never popular in Britain – this is the only print in which he appears – and by way of dismissal Robert Walpole's famous comment, 'Every man has his price', is scrawled across the print.

A Representation of the Figures exhibited and paraded through the Streets of Philadelphia on Saturday, the 30th of September, 1780

The *Pennsylvania Gazette* in November carried this condemnation of Arnold's treachery. As the traitor was safe in New York the citizens of Philadelphia, where Arnold had been the Governor, had to make do with a two-faced effigy on his way to the gallows. The Devil is driving the wagon to the eternal flames of damnation and he holds a purse to remind the crowd that Arnold, like Judas, betrayed his leader for money – £6,000.

The words accompanying this print assert that the discovery of his treachery was due to the 'Omniscient Creator'. So God was on the side of the Americans, but in fact the discovery was due to the pure fluke and misfortune of Major André blundering into a patrol of three Americans soldiers whom he thought to be British.

Chapter Nine

The Generals

*'I do not know whether our generals will frighten the enemy,
but I know they frighten me when I think of them.'* Lord North

BRITAIN LOST THE WAR BECAUSE the politicians in London failed to grasp the fundamental change that the rebels wanted; failed to pursue a consistent policy; failed to commit the necessary resources of cash and men, and failed to realise that it was impossible to 'conquer' the vast territory of America. Britain also lost the war because the three generals — Howe, Burgoyne, and Clinton — were utterly inadequate and each had character flaws that led to them throwing away time and again the chance of destroying Washington's army. In 1776 Major Charles Stuart, one of Bute's sons who was serving in the 37th Regiment, summed them up as 'a pack of the most ordinary men who gave themselves trouble about the merest trifles, whilst things of consequence go unresponded.' Lord North was, as we have seen, bluntly frank.

THOMAS GAGE (1720-1789) Commander-in-Chief, 1773-1775

A Political Lesson
7 September 1774
J Dixon

In this allegory America the horse while on the road to Boston – just VI miles away – has thrown its rider the Massachusetts Governor, General Gage. In order to punish Boston, Gage had moved the state legislature in June to Salem and this persuaded Massachusetts to send five representatives to a General Congress and a Solemn League and Covenant – reminiscent of the English Civil War – pledged to stop all trade with Britain until the Boston Port Bill was repealed. Gage was married to an American and had much sympathy with the colonists, but his advice to London was generally ignored; he recommended the repeal of all the Coercive Acts – that was to become London's official policy three years later. In the defence of Boston he made two strategic mistakes: first by abandoning Charleston peninsula and, second, by allowing the rebels to place their cannons on Dorchester Heights. He had to suffer the first major reverse of the war – the evacuation of Boston – and that cost him his job.

A POLITICAL LESSON.

The CATCH SINGERS.

SIR WILLIAM HOWE
1776

The Catch Singers

These are four of the greatest supporters for the war drinking to success. Lord North, on the right; next to him is Lord George Germain, the Secretary of State for the Colonies since November 1775; seated next to him is Lord Sandwich, the first Lord of the Admiralty who was the 'soul' of the actual Catch Club, but it could also be Vice-Admiral Lord Howe, who was appointed Commander-in-Chief of North America in February 1776. The soldier on the left in military uniform and high boots is Sir William Howe, Admiral Howe's brother, who had been appointed as commander of the army in October 1775. They are all utterly confident that Britain would bring America to heel – it was merely a question of time. They all have moneybags and Sir William Howe confidently boasts, 'Ha, he, he, we have fill'd our bags with gold'.

HOWE had the virtue of being a good field commander in a set battle. He emerged the pyrrhic victor at Bunker Hill and he then outmanoeuvred and beat Washington at Brooklyn Heights, Harlem Heights, White Plains and Brandywine. But he failed utterly to follow up the advantage by pursuing a demoralised rebel army – a rag bag of volunteers – in full flight. This hesitancy, the lack of a killer instinct, destroyed the morale of his own army, as there was no decisive blow after a series of victories.

Howe was lazy, dull, distant and semi-detached. A Captain Hammond visited his flagship to discuss the strategic move to Philadelphia only to find him still in bed at 10 o'clock in the morning. His reputation for lethargy was reinforced by suspending all operations during the winter, preferring instead the warmth, comfort and conviviality of Philadelphia and the charms of his American mistress, Mrs Joshua Loring; the rebels sang to the tune of Yankee Doodle:

> *Sir William he, smug as a flea,*
> *Lay all this time a-snoring,*
> *Nor dreamed of harm as he lay warm*
> *In bed with Mrs Loring.*

Another wag suggested, after Washington's crossing of the Delaware on his way to Trenton, that Howe should be elevated as Lord Delay-Warr. He failed to support Burgoyne, and spent the rest of his life justifying this neglect. A poor military decision, but there was vanity as well – he wanted to be the general who administered the knock-out blow rather than the dilettante, swaggering playboy from London.

His mission was cursed from the start as he had asked George III not only to command the British army in America but also to negotiate a peaceful solution. Generals make poor diplomats for their task is to win not to parley; negotiation for Howe meant for the Americans a total surrender. On his return to London the Whigs savaged him, and the government wanted a scapegoat, but a parliamentary inquiry was inconclusive. He published his defence in 1780 but lost his seat in Parliament at the election later that year.

CLINTON Howe resigned his command and was succeeded in May 1778 by General Henry Clinton who had served alongside him for the previous three years. He still regarded his job as the suppression of a rebellion rather than to wage war, and so there was a certain fastidious holding back. Charles Stuart said that he was not up to commanding a troop of horse. Admiral Rodney in New York wrote to Germain:

> *'You must not expect an end of the American war till you can find*
> *a general of active spirit, and who hates the Americans from principle.*
> *Such a man with the sword of war and justice on his side will do*
> *wonders; for in this war I am convinced the sword should cut deep.'*

SIR HENRY CLINTON Commander-in-Chief, 1778-1781
He does not appear in any caricature but this print was published in November 1778.

Rodney went on to suggest that Benedict Arnold would be a better commander-in-chief. Clinton complained constantly about not having enough men. When Washington was in trouble, facing mutinies in his army, Clinton moaned again to Eden, 'For God's sake send us money, men, and provisions, or expect nothing but complaints. Send out another admiral or let me go home.' But his army amounted to 30,000 British troops, 8,000 Hessians, and loyalists could muster up to 8,000. He must also bear some of the blame for Saratoga through his delay in marching north to help Burgoyne, and again in 1781 he delayed in mounting the expedition to save Cornwallis at Yorktown.

Indecisive, apprehensive, and lacking in confidence, he dithered and dallied. His letters to his ministers and friends at home were full of whining and self-pity, but he drew some comfort from his pretty mistress in New York, Mrs Mary Baddeley, and from his salary of £12,500 which was much higher than North's.

GENERAL JOHNNY BURGOYNE
Le général burgoyne à Saratoga

In this French print, which appeared later, Burgoyne is depicted as a shackled turkey restrained by a soldier holding a stick in its beak. He should never have been listened to in London by Germain and North, and never entrusted to command an expedition in a country and over a terrain of which he had no knowledge or experience. He was an amateur soldier when what was needed were all the professional skills to organise a thorough campaign, to encourage more loyalists to rally to his banner, to hold his Native Indian allies steadfast and above all to establish an effective supply line to provide food, clothes and ammunition for his soldiers. Once again Britain had a general who took his cellar and his mistress with him on the campaign. The surrender at Saratoga was the turning point – every single American knew that Britain could be beaten.

LORD CORNWALLIS
Le Lord Cornwallis
1781

This French caricature bears no resemblance to the British general. He is depicted as a scrawny little runt but he was florid and heavily built – the French wanted to gloat. Cornwallis' reputation was not diminished by the war – he always seemed to get a good press. Personally brave – his horse was once shot from under him – but his record was chequered. He was outwitted by Washington at Princeton; victory at Guilford Courthouse was won by his command to fire cannon into the fighting troops killing some of his own men; but beating Gates at Camden was a triumph. His march into Virginia was reckless and he shares the blame for the surrender of Yorktown with Clinton, though Clinton was made the scapegoat. On his return to London in January 1782 as a prisoner on parole he was chaired around Exeter, but he finally came to the right judgement: 'The conquest of America by fire and sword is not to be accomplished let your numbers be what they may.' He went on to greater things – Governor-General in India and elevated from an earl to a marquis. Not everyone agreed and in a verse the *London Courant* did not let him escape:

When southward, Cornwallis first entered the land
As Commander-in-Chief, with the sword in his hand,
He swaggered and boasted, and threaten'd the fates
That in spite of their teeth he would ravage the States.

Le Lord Cornwallia
sortant des Carolines après y avoir
été Longtems Ressere.

Lor-d Am^{hers}-t on Duty.

If I had Power,
I'd kill 20 in an Hour,

LORD AMHERST L—d Am----t on Duty
12 June 1780
Matthew Darly

Lord Amherst was nominally Commander-in-Chief from 1778 but he had little influence on the American war. He had served successfully in America in the Seven Years War being responsible for the successful invasion of Canada. He had however a low opinion of Americans, 'if left to themselves would eat fried pork and lay in their beds all day long'. As for the Cherokees, they were a 'perfidious race of Savages'. In the Indian wars of 1764-1765, he was one of the first commanders to use germ warfare as he sanctioned giving Indians blankets contaminated with smallpox.

Here he is shown suppressing the Gordon Riots in 1780 – successfully cutting down geese.

Veluti in Speculum – Just in Observation (below)
1782

The Devil invites the British generals to look into the mirror to see their own image and to accept responsibility for the humiliating debacle. They were led by Amherst; behind him scratching his chin is General Murray who lost Minorca; behind him is Burgoyne; then the plumper Cornwallis; Howe looking over his shoulder; the diminutive Tarleton and then Clinton.

LORD DUNMORE

'The most formidable Enemy America has' – Washington

The Royal Governor of Virginia, Lord Dunmore, hit upon a brilliant idea to defeat the American rebels. In November 1775 he issued a proclamation that freed 'all indentured Servants, Negroes or others (appertaining to Rebels)' provided that they were 'able and willing to bear Arms for his Majesty's troops'. In a tobacco state that depended upon slave labour this appalled the colony's American estate owners and provoked from Washington an angry condemnation: 'If the Virginians are wise, that Arch Traitor to the Rights of Humanity, Lord Dunmore, should be instantly crushed, if it takes the force of the whole colony to do so.'

Dunmore's imaginative strike increased his force within a month from 300 to 600, one of whom was a servant from Washington's own estate of Mount Vernon. Washington was very wary of Dunmore. His regiment dubbed 'the Ethiopian' included 800 black labourers and emblazoned across their chests were the words, 'Liberty to Slaves'. What destroyed this brilliant coup was smallpox. Dunmore's troops in the early months of 1776 were decimated by smallpox among their ranks. Hundreds died and it reduced his capacity to fight. By July the Ethiopian regiment had fallen to 300 men who had to take refuge on ships, 'Lord Dunmore's pestilential fleet'. So a brilliant initiative was defeated not by American arms but by the Variola virus.

GEORGE WASHINGTON (1732-1799) fought alongside the British against the French and the Indians in the Seven Years War. He failed to resist an attack on Fort Necessity where many of his 400 men were sick or underfed and after a day's fighting he had to capitulate. He later told his brother that his time spent as a soldier was the worst experience of his life.

In 1763 he returned to his family's plantation in Virginia which was sustained by slave labour. He became, partly through his marriage to Martha Custis, a widow whose husband had left her very well-off, one of the wealthiest men in America and was able to live the life of an English country gentleman – clothed and booted by London tradesmen; owning a substantial country mansion; with his devotion to hunting making him one of the best horsemen in Virginia – becoming a member of the local legislature and a delegate to the Continental Congress in 1775.

Its main task was to forge unity among the different colonies by agreeing to establish and fund an army, and then to appoint a commander-in-chief. John Hancock, the wealthy and arrogant young merchant from Boston expected to be chosen, since the first battle with the enemy had taken place in Massachusetts. John Adams decided that the cause did not need a Boston firebrand who had never served in any army, but a gent from the southern state of Virginia who had had some military experience in the Seven Years War, and he nominated George Washington – a tall, quiet, grave, aloof, modest but commanding figure who had had the good sense to turn up in military uniform. Hancock glared and fumed but it was the most crucial decision taken in America during the revolution. One man, Sam Adams, started the revolution; it was left to George Washington to take it to victory.

John Adams said of him, 'he was always the tallest man in the room'. He was more than that: he was highly intelligent, dogged, determined and a first class administrator, but he was no wordsmith and rather unimaginative. He was not a politician and held the members of Congress in little more than contempt, confiding to his diary in 1776: 'Chimney corner patriots abound; venality, corruption, prostitution of office for selfish ends, abuse of trust, perversion of funds from a natural to a private use, and speculations upon the necessities of the times pervade all interest.'

Between 1776-77 Washington ensured that the revolution did not collapse by keeping his army together after a series of humiliating defeats. For a time the revolution was Washington and the army. In the ensuing year he fashioned a professional army but he was never prepared to risk it in a full-scale battle with the British. Time and again his caution led to no engagements and this annoyed John Adams who openly condemned him in September 1777, 'I am sick of Fabian systems in all quarters…My toast is a short and robust war.' In 1778 and 1779 General Clinton fretted over his inability to draw Washington into battle and in November 1779 he reported his frustration (but also partly as an excuse for his own conduct): 'He still keeps at a great distance from us and so near to the [Watchung] mountains that a few hours puts him into them out of reach, indeed the greatest part of his army is still behind the mountains.' This tactic worked for the three British generals, Howe, Clinton and Cornwallis were never able to draw him into a major engagement.

George Washington
1776
Artist unknown
The author found this print, which has not hitherto been published, in a New York bookshop. The bookseller thought it might have been a label that was stuck on kegs of gunpowder.

The Protector of his COUNTRY   The Supporter of LIBERTY And the Benefactor of Mankind

The American Armies in chief of the Commander Esqr WASHINGTON GEORGE Excellency His

May his name never be forgotten

COLONEL ARNOLD.
Who Commanded the Provincial Troops sent against QUEBEC, through the Wilderness of Canada, and was Wounded in Storming that City, under General Montgomery.
London Published as the Act directs 26 March 1776 by Thos Hart

THE GLORIOUS WASHINGTON AND GATES
1778
The Boston Almanack

This is the one of the very few contemporary woodcuts of Washington – on the left – and it appeared in the patriotic journal, *The Boston Almanack*. The portraits are not caricatures. It is interesting that at this stage Gates is shown alongside Washington – it wasn't just a one man show.

BENEDICT ARNOLD
A British print after his defection in 1780

The best fighting commander in either army. Formerly a British soldier, he joined the militia ten days after Lexington and proposed to Washington a two-pronged attack on Canada. He led 1,100 men in an epic 350-mile march from the coast through the forests of Maine to arrive at Quebec – his men were reduced to eating pet dogs. In a blinding snowstorm he joined in the attack upon Quebec and he received a wound in his right knee. In 1777 he was the inspiration behind the defeat of Burgoyne at Saratoga, although Gates got the credit. A monument on the battlefield of Saratoga is shaped in a boot in recognition of a leg injury and 'in memory of the most brilliant soldier of the Continental Army'. Overlooked by Congress for promotion he became Governor of Philadelphia in 1778 and while he was there he began the process of detachment from the American cause that led in 1780 to him going over to the British. He led successful and daring raids into Chesapeake Bay in 1780 but after the defeat he went to Britain where he was not rewarded with a military post. He died in 1801 a broken and poor man. In American history he is the arch-traitor; but Washington failed to make greater use of his genius for fighting and winning.

GENERAL CHARLES LEE

'A sarcastic genius' – Tom Paine

A soldier since the age of 14 and a lieutenant at 21, Lee had fought in Portugal, Poland, Russia and America. After killing a man in a duel in Italy he fled to England where he attacked the authority of George III, calling him a 'despicable, stupid, not innoxious dolt' and in October 1773 decided to go to America again. He soon moved into the circle of Hancock, Adams and Washington becoming in 1775 major general. Washington held him in high regard: 'He is the first officer in military knowledge and experience we have in the whole army.' He was eccentric – surrounded by dogs; razor-thin and acerbic; violently unpredictable; excessively vain; insatiably ambitious, and headstrong. He married the daughter of a Seneca chief and was given the Mohawk name, Qunewaterike or Boiling Water.

When Washington was in full flight across New Jersey after losing Fort Washington and Fort Lee, Lee intrigued with Washington's own secretary, bad-mouthed him to his friends in Congress, and even plotted to succeed him. He deplored Washington's indecisiveness, confiding to Bowdon, President of the Massachusetts Council, 'there are times we must commit treason against the laws of the State, for the salvation of the State'.

Lee's dream of replacing Washington was finished on 13 December 1776 when a troop of horses led by another colourful figure, Banastre Tarleton, had come upon Lee breakfasting alone, away from his army, and took him prisoner. It was just as well for Washington that Lee was captured because after his breakfast he had dictated a letter to Gates in which he commented scathingly on the disaster at Fort Washington and continued, 'entrez–nous a certain great man is damnably deficient – he has thrown me into a situation where I have no choice of difficulties – if I stay in this province I will risk myself and army, if I do not stay the province is lost for ever.' Lee remained a prisoner until he was exchanged in April 1778. Later he was disgraced by Washington for his conduct in the battle of Monmouth Courthouse.

HORATIO GATES (1728–1806) had been lucky to be appointed the commander at Saratoga as most believed that Benedict Arnold had played the decisive role in Burgoyne's defeat. Gates was the 'politician's general', undermining Washington's position through his friends in Congress. When Congress appointed him Commander-in-Chief of the Southern Army his friend, General Lee, said 'Take care lest your Northern laurels turn into Southern willows'. His defeat in the battle of Camden in August 1780 ended his career – he panicked and fled.

General Charles Lee

NATHANAEL GREENE (1740-1786) (left)
Turned down as an officer because of a limp, he offered to serve in the ranks and his persistence led to him becoming a brigadier general in Rhode Island. Thought to be one of Washington's best generals, but he was absent at Brooklyn Heights; abandoned his men in the unholdable Fort Washington; faltered at Germantown; and as commander in the southern campaign he lost several engagements in spite of having a larger army. But, at Valley Forge he really saved the American army by planning the proper supply of food, clothes, weapons and ammunition. He was second to Washington who recognised his ability, 'There is not an officer of the Army, nor a man in America, more sincerely attached to the interests of this country.' After the war the state of Georgia gave him a cotton plantation and he died there suddenly of sunstroke.

Chapter Ten

American Forces

'I dare say these men would fight very well (if properly officered) although they are exceedingly dirty and nasty people.' Washington

BEFORE THE REVOLUTION EVERY ADULT MALE, apart from Quakers in Pennsylvania, had to take part by law in military exercises each year. This resulted in virtually every American having a gun which they had been trained to use. One English MP, Charles Memish, said in 1778 that 'the Americans had one advantage in their militia over most nations: the constant use of the firelock from children.' Many were also skilled marksmen since they shot for the table, and hiding behind trees and boulders they were able to pick-off the British redcoats. Burgoyne, writing later about his defeat at the Battle of Bemis Heights in 1777, commented upon the riflemen under the command of Daniel Morgan: 'The enemy had with their Army a great number of marksmen, armed with rifle barrel pieces: these, during an engagement, hovered upon the flanks in small detachments, and were very expert in securing themselves and in shifting their ground. In this action many placed themselves in high trees in the rear of their own line, and there was seldom a minute's interval of smoke in any part of our line without officers being taken off by a single shot.' In June 1778 Thomas Jefferson claimed that American losses were lower than the British because 'every soldier in our army has been intimate with his gun from his infancy'.

THIRTY SIX-SHILLINGS.

Issued in defence of American Liberty.

Ense petit placidam sub Libertate. Quietem.

Decm.r 7. 1775.

American Soldiers Notes
7 December 1775
Paul Revere

After Congress had decided to recruit an army it had to settle on how to pay them. They commissioned Paul Revere to design and print 'Soldiers Notes' of various denominations which started at six shillings that were in effect IOUs which could be cashed one day for money. The printing was closely supervised by officials and they all had to be countersigned. Each carried the defiant phrase, 'Issued in defence of American liberty' and the Latin phrase, *Ense petit placidam sub Libertate Quietem* – which means, 'With the sword he seeks tranquillity under Liberty' and 'Quiet'. A tax had to be levied to meet the payment of these notes. As this paper money was over-issued its value slumped and soldiers, even when they got them which was not regularly, felt cheated.

So when the word went out in Massachusetts that volunteers were needed to drive the British out of Boston, a militia army of 20,000 quickly emerged. This force was composed of farmers, store-keepers, clerks, hunters, carpenters, farriers, smiths – they had no uniform, only coats or fringed buckskin shirts and their main weapon was the long Kentucky rifle. All these men had other jobs; the harvest had to be garnered and they did not care for soldiering-on during the long, cold winters. Washington welcomed them but he knew their disadvantages: 'They come in, you cannot tell how; go, you cannot tell when; and act, you cannot tell where; consume your provisions, exhaust your stores, and leave you at last at the critical moments.' They were, however, a constant feature of both the northern and the southern campaigns. In the southern campaign they assumed virtually the nature of robber-bands with strong local leaders like Sumter and Morgan who evoked great personal loyalty. They followed largely their own interests which frustrated the commander, and Nathanael Greene who, when he took over command in the south in November 1780, likened them to 'the locusts of Egypt'.

American officers like Colonel Otho Williams were scathing about the militia's ability to withstand an attack. His comment on Camden was: 'The infamous cowardice of the militia from Virginia and North Carolina gave the enemy every advantage over our regular troops.' The militia did provide one vitally important element in the defeat of the British army: they ensured that battle after battle, the British could not consolidate and extend their control of the surrounding countryside where the militia could disappear and then suddenly reappear.

Washington realised that he needed a regular, well-trained professional army to take on and defeat the British. He began to fashion this in the siege of Boston and in 1777 during the cold, hard winter of Valley Forge he was helped by the German von Steuben who instilled a sense of discipline and regular drilling. The army at that time had shrunk to just a few hundred men for of the soldiers who were supposed to enlist for three years many left in the autumn, preferring their own homes to the hardship of camp life, and only some returned in the spring. Desertion was rife and half the men who were recruited simply faded away, but among those who stayed were the junior officers and NCOs who had seen battle and survived, and were ready to fight again.

Washington had to cope with poor equipment and poor supplies. Time and again he wrote to Congress about the lack of shoes and stockings for his men. In some years the soldiers had no boots or coats and only meagre supplies of food which led some of the men to mutiny during 1779-81. Washington was quite ruthless in putting them down: he shot two of the ringleaders. General Wayne was rather more sympathetic and said his men were 'poorly clothed, badly fed, and worse paid, some of them having not received a paper dollar for nearly

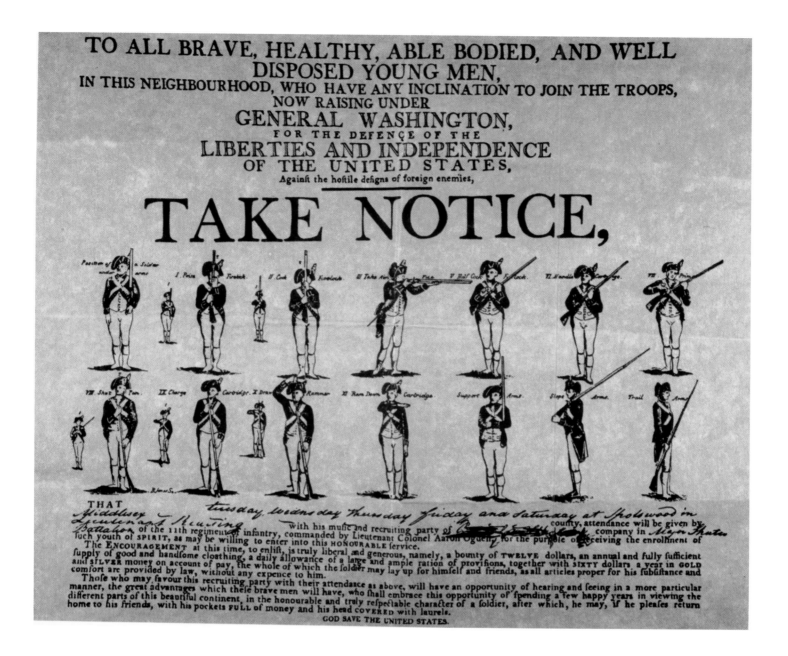

TO ALL BRAVE, HEALTHY, ABLE BODIED, AND WELL
DISPOSED YOUNG MEN,
IN THIS NEIGHBOURHOOD, WHO HAVE ANY INCLINATION TO JOIN THE TROOPS,
NOW RAISING UNDER
GENERAL WASHINGTON,
FOR THE DEFENCE OF THE
LIBERTIES AND INDEPENDENCE
OF THE UNITED STATES,
Against the hostile designs of foreign enemies,

TAKE NOTICE,

A recruiting hand-bill

twelve months; exposed to winters, piercing cold to drifting snows and chilling blasts with no protection but old worn-out coats, tattered linen overalls and but one blanket between three men.' Even as late as 1781, the year of victory for America, Washington admitted, 'instead of having magazines full of provisions we have scanty presence scattered here and in the different states. Instead of arsenals well supplied with military stores they are poorly provided…in a word instead of having everything in readiness to take the field, we have nothing, and instead of having the prospect of a glorious and offensive campaign before us we have a bewildered and gloomily defensive one, unless we should receive a powerful aide of ships, land troops and money from our generous allies.' It was a better army than the rag tail one that besieged Boston in 1776 but it was still very far from an effective fighting force.

The French were contemptuous of the American army. A French soldier who had served in the failed Franco-

From the beginning Washington wanted recruits to the Continental Army for such regulars would be better trained and more committed than the local militias. Here he offers 'a bounty of TWELVE dollars…and SIXTY dollars a year in GOLD' as well as 'handsome clothing…and a large and ample ration of provisions'. Recruiting promises were like pie crusts, made to be broken. Time and again Washington had to beg Congress for more money for his soldiers' clothes and often foraging parties had to rob local farms whether they supported the rebels or not. In 1777 Congress imposed conscription but even then Washington had to appeal to the separate states for men and supplies.

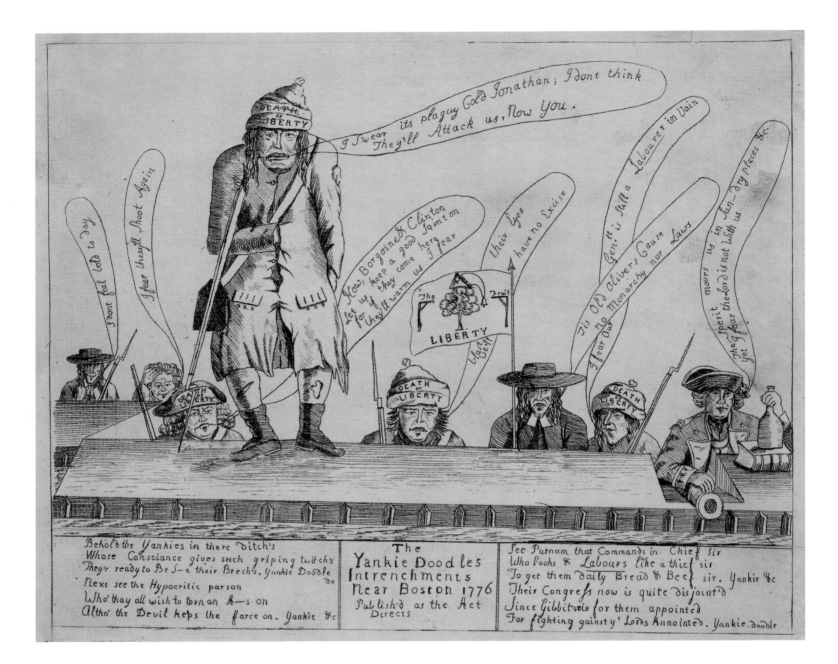

The Yankee Doodles Intrenchments near Boston
1776

This is one of the few anti-American prints. The rag-tag, bob-tail army of Washington is shown in a sorry state. The American general on the right is Israel Putnam who is depicted as defeatist and finding consolation in a bottle. Washington's army was formed by groups of volunteers: there was no uniform, no willingness to obey orders and a strong desire to return to their farms. Washington deplored the 'dirty mercenary spirit that pervades the whole' and at one point he said if he had known how bad they were he would never have accepted their command. The English too had little regard for the patriots: General Burgoyne called them 'peasants', 'ragamuffins' and a 'rabble-in-arms'. During the long siege of Boston Washington fashioned these volunteers from the states into a fighting force: he imposed discipline, issued daily orders for the first time and fought strenuously to get better weapons and equipment.

Regimental flag of the Philadelphia Light Horse Troop

American siege of Rhode Island in 1778 was in no doubt about their quality:

'All the tailors and apothecaries in the country must have been called out, I should think. One could recognise them by their round wigs. They were mounted on bad nags and looked like a flock of ducks in cross belts. The infantry was no better than the cavalry and appeared to be cut after the same pattern.'

At the beginning of the war, British officers also did not conceal their contempt for the rebel forces. Captain William Leslie was part of the British force that sprang a surprise landing in September 1776 in East Manhattan (roughly where the United Nations building is today) and caused the rebel forces to flee. His comment was that to him the rebels 'are so out generaled that it is impossible for them to know where to prepare for defence…the rogues have not learnt manners yet, they cannot look gentlemen in the face.' Later when he captured some Americans he reported that 'the poor infatuated wretches we took were most all drunk, even the officers'.

The Continental Army at Yorktown (above)
1781

This is a sketch by a French officer who fought at Yorktown. On the right there is an artilleryman standing besides a rifleman in militia/frontiersman dress, next is an infantryman in full uniform, and finally a black private of the Rhode Island Regiment. By this time, Washington's army was a much more organised professional force and it included former slaves. At Yorktown, a German captain observed that a quarter of the Continental Army was African American, and he described the Rhode Island Regiment as 'the most neatly dressed, the best under arms, and the most precise in its manoeuvres'.

American soldiers as seen by the Germans (right)

The engraver depended upon hearsay, but much is right: fringed jackets of buckskin; short caps and one without shoes. When a soldier deserted, adverts were put in the press offering a reward and describing the soldiers' dress and appearance, and several stated that the deserters had no shoes or stockings.

An American Dragoon 1775 (opposite)

Washington's army had four regiments of cavalry amounting to one thousand men. They barely featured in the northern campaigns but came into their own in the south with lightning raids and fast-moving skirmishes. The distinctive dragoon helmet was a protection against sabre slashes during a cavalry attack.

Chapter Eleven

The British Army

'We get terrible provisions…putrid meat and wormy biscuits that have spoiled on the ships. Many of them have taken sick with…the bloody flux and diarrhoea. Foul fever is spreading…we have little rest night and day.'
A British soldier at the Siege of Yorktown, October 1781

THE FIRST PERIL THAT A SOLDIER FACED was the sea voyage to America, for the conditions on board were appalling. One corporal summed it up: 'There was continual destruction in the foretop, the pox above-abound, the plague between decks, hell in the forecastle, the devil at the helm.' In the period 1776-1780, 8,437 soldiers were embarked for the West Indies but only 7,500 arrived as 932 had died in passage.

In the 1770s the British army had commitments across the world. In 1776 25,000 soldiers served in Britain; 8,000 in Ireland; 5,000 in Gibraltar; 4,000 in Africa and the West Indies; 14,000 in Canada; and Howe had under his command 40,000. Up until Saratoga there were few recruits – indeed only one new regiment was added to the army. After France entered the war, recruitment was stepped up – 12 regiments were added – and by 1781 the army had increased to 110,000 men with 56,000 of them in America. In addition, there were 13,000 Hessians and throughout the war the German mercenaries contributed between a third and a quarter of the British strength.

3 Shillings a Day. 2 Shillings a Day. 1 Shilling a Day. **SIX-PENCE A DAY.** Yankees. Fire and Water. Sword and Famine.

This Sketch displays the Hardship a Soldier and his Family endure on the bare Subsistance of Sixpence a Day, while the lowest Trades earn sufficient to enjoy the Comforts of Life.

Published 26. Oct.t 1775 by W. Humphrey, Garrard Street, Soho.

Six-Pence a Day
October 1775

Britain was not finding it easy to recruit soldiers and this anti-recruiting print was no help. The soldier's wife, barefoot, ragged and pregnant, asks what is to become of their children. The state of the emaciated recruit contrasts with the plump sedan-chair man who earned three shillings a day; the coachman at two shillings a day; and the sweeper at one shilling.

The effective fighting force was much less as illness – diarrhoea, scurvy, smallpox and various marsh fevers akin to malaria – took their toll. The other problem was that detachments had to be spread out over the colonies to hold the position in loyalist towns. This meant that, for example, at Saratoga there were only 3,250 British troops (and 3,000 Hessians); at the victory of Camden in 1780, Cornwallis had 2,043 men and when he surrendered in Yorktown in 1781 he had 6,000 Britons, of which only 3,273 were fit for duty. Time and time again, Gage, Howe and Clinton begged Germain in London to send them more men, but very few arrived. Indeed on France's entry into the war, Clinton was ordered to send 5,000 men – ten regiments – to the West Indies. In February 1779 Clinton commented on the fact that he had 36,000 men, 'but by detachments, etc., I am reduced to little more than 18,000 men, a great proportion are foreigners and provincials'.

Each general hoped that loyalist militia would rally to the cause and some did, but not in the numbers they expected. They never really managed to secure the regular commitment of loyalists who were prepared to serve continuously under British command. Cornwallis in the south was disappointed not only with the number of loyalists but also with 'their supiness and pusillanimity'. But the English high command did not really appreciate the sacrifice and commitment expected from loyalist volunteers. One recorded:

'A dissatisfaction prevailed at this moment amongst the militia founded on General Clinton's hand-bill which requires everyman that having but three children and every single man to do six months' duty out of their own province when required. This appeared like compulsion, instead of acting voluntarily…and they were inconsequence ready to give up the cause.'

Some of the loyalist units were merged into the British Legion which became a six-troop light dragoon regiment. Lieutenant-Colonel Simcoe, who had fought at Boston and been wounded at Brandywine, and was one of the most resourceful British commanders, formed the Queen's Rangers which became in 1779 the first American regiment. It had one Light, one Grenadier, one Highland, eight rifle companies and three troops of Light Dragoons. They played an important part in the successes of the southern campaign.

Most of the Native American Indian tribes preferred the distant British to the local American land-grabbers but their actual involvement was uncertain and sporadic. In the Carolinas, a few freed negro slaves took up arms with the British and called themselves 'The King of England's Soldiers'. All this was a very different picture from India where the British army in 1782 amounted to 115,000 men, 90% of them being Indians.

The main force consisted of infantry regiments: the Grenadiers, riflemen who were also trained to throw grenades, hence their narrow hats; and Light Infantry, who were principally marksmen operating on the flank. They were supported by companies of artillery and at Yorktown there were sixty-four cannon. Only two cavalry regiments – the 16th and 17th Light Dragoons – served in America, as transporting horses from Britain was a nightmare for few survived the sea crossing. In 1777, when Howe moved his army from New York to Chesapeake Bay by sea, most of his horses had to be destroyed because of the rough weather. Through the war, there was four times the number of cavalry troops in Britain than in America.

TRUCRO DUCE NIL DESPERANDOM.

First Battalion of PENNSYLVANIA LOYALISTS, commanded by His Excellency Sir WILLIAM HOWE, K. B.

ALL INTREPID ABLE-BODIED

HEROES.

WHO are willing to serve His MAJESTY KING GEORGE the Third, in Defence of their Country, Laws and Conftitution, againft the arbitrary Ufurpations of a tyrannical Congrefs, have now not only an Opportunity of manifefting their Spirit, by affifting in reducing to Obedience their too-long deluded Countrymen, but alfo of acquiring the polite Accomplifhments of a Soldier, by ferving only two Years, or during the prefent Rebellion in America.

Such fpirited Fellows, who are willing to engage, will be rewarded at the End of the War, befides their Laurels, with 50 Acres of Land, where every gallant Hero may retire, and enjoy his Bottle and Lafs.

Each Volunteer will receive as a Bounty, FIVE DOLLARS, befides Arms, Cloathing and Accoutrements, and every other Requifite proper to accommodate a Gentleman Soldier, by applying to Lieutenant Colonel ALLEN, or at Captain KEARNY's Rendezvous, at PATRICK TONRY's, three Doors above Market-ftreet, in Second-ftreet.

British Recruiting Poster

Britain needed the help of loyalist soldiers. The most reliable research has identified forty-one loyalist regiments amounting to some 19,000 men. They were raised locally and most effective in skirmishing and smaller engagements. There were some famous regimental names – Royal Americans, Butler's Rangers and the King's Royal Regiment, and two loyalist regiments who were very active in the southern campaigns – the Royal Highland Emigrants and the Volunteers of Ireland became regular units of the British infantry.

This appeal from Sir William Howe is directed to 'spirited Fellows' who would be rewarded with fifty acres and 'his Bottle and Lass'.

A Recruiting Bill Board (left)

This wooden life-size recruiting figure would have been propped up outside a recruiting centre to attract the attention of passers-by. Such figures had been used in the Jacobite Rebellion and in the Seven Years War, and this one is attributed to 1768.

QUALIFYING for a CAMPAIN.

London, Printed for R. Sayer & J. Bennett. Map & Printsellers N°.53 Fleet Street, as the Act directs 4 June 1777.

Verney delin.

Qualifying for a Campain
4 June 1777

As this print was published before the battle of Saratoga, it became a much more eloquent comment after the defeat that September. The British troops gossip in a relaxed way; fence with buttoned foils in hideous and cowardly postures; fire upon a castle of cards; and the only target they can hit is a tethered cat: not even the dog can be provoked to kill the rat that goads it. People in London were getting fed-up with a war that was going nowhere, but one in which Britain had a better-trained and a better-equipped army.

The woods, hills and rivers in the north meant that most engagements were the task of infantrymen – many in close hand-to-hand fighting with bayonets and swords. The success of the British army after Boston was in large part due to changing the three-rank line to a form of two ranks: the rear men covering the gaps of the first rank. This was the birth of 'the thin red line' but it required discipline and coolness to operate successfully.

The war in the southern states from 1780 was quite different. There were no hedges, few walls, and the country was open, but interspersed with swamps and marshes. As a result, the light cavalry came into their own, and there were a series of lightning skirmishes and bush fights by mounted troops who carried flintlock carbines, pistols and swords. Most of these soldiers were local militia men with their own horses.

The main weapon was the Brown Bess flintlock musket which had been in service as the army's principal weapon since 1717. It was very effective up to a range of about 100 yards, but was cumbersome to load – twelve separate movements were necessary, but the most experienced soldiers could fire off several one ounce lead balls in a minute. But Britain passed up the chance to adopt a new rifle invented by Major Patrick

ADVANCE *THREE STEPS* BACKWARDS. *(View of command the last War by Col.*
OR THE MILITIA HEROES.

Pub. by Darlys Strand.

Ferguson which had a breech-loading system. A Ferguson was able to fire four rounds a minute for five minutes, and it could be loaded from a kneeling or lying position. In America, Ferguson formed his own company of experienced marksmen and it was highly successful, but, after he was badly wounded at Brandywine, Howe disbanded it because it had been raised without his knowledge.

As the Recruitment Acts of 1778 and 1789 allowed the conscription of the unemployed and criminals, prisons were a good recruiting ground as convicted criminals were pardoned on enlistment. Recruits were given a shilling to drink King George's health and a bounty of £3 to serve three years. All the officers had to buy their commission and they learnt the art of warfare by practical experience on the battlefield. Several of the senior officers had risen to their position through local politics and retained their positions as Members of Parliament.

Washington envied the drill and discipline of the British forces. He recognised that they were a superior fighting force and that is why he spent much of the war avoiding an open confrontation with them. The war was lost not by the British soldiers but by their generals.

Advance three steps Backwards, or the Militia Heroes
1779
M Darly

The French entry into the war in 1778 and Spain's in 1779 raised the very real threat of invasion, not in America but in the south of England. Both countries wanted to crush England and Britain's response was in true Falstaffian style as it prepared to defend itself. Darly could not resist showing the British territorial army of the late 18th century as disorganised, untrained, hapless and hopeless. England certainly needed a gale to disperse the Franco-Spanish invasion fleet.

A contemporary poem:
Can we Invasions dred, when volunteers
Like these propose to fight the Gay Monsieurs?
Certainly No! Such Taylors, Coblers, Bakers,
Always must Conquer, led by Engine Makers.

Recrues Angolia Partant Pour L'Amerique
1780

This is a French copy of a print by Bunbury that first appeared in
1770. The recruits are a poor bunch, scrawny, weedy, slow-witted
and detached. The French, still smarting from their defeat by Britain
in the Seven Years War (1756-1763) were only too glad to re-
discover and gloat over this old caricature.

THE WARLEY HEROES OR THE LIGHT INFANTRY ON FULL MARCH.

The Warley Heroes or the Light Infantry on Full March
1778

When France declared war England prepared to meet an invasion. In 1779 there was a French army of 50,000 near Calais which Lafayette joined. Militia forces were raised all over the country – not just in the south east, for Manchester mustered 1,000. From 1778-1780 two camps were set up: one at Warley Common in Essex and another at Cox Heath, Kent. Both became visitor attractions for families seeking reassurance that they would be protected – at least after a fashion.

The Queen's Rangers (right)

Simcoe commanded this corps of loyalist troops and wrote its history in 1781, a copy of which he presented to George III. This was the most distinguished of the five provincial units recognised in 1779 in the newly created American Army Establishment. The Queen's Rangers became the First American Regiment.

PRISONERS IN AMERICA

During the war prisoners were a burden for whoever captured them and that led to many wounded prisoners being killed off on the battlefield. In the battles for New York, Howe instructed his men to use their bayonets – a euphemism for killing any men taken. Medical services, being inadequate and primitive, naturally dealt with their own wounded first. A prisoner was just another mouth to feed, another body to be clothed and another enemy to be watched and controlled. The British took only soldiers of the Continental Army as prisoners and some were persuaded to join the British army – some even being sent to the West Indies.

American Prisoners
Drawing by John Trumbull

Prisoners were an expensive burden. After the surrender of Charleston in 1779, some 2,000 American prisoners were kept in prison hulks. An American surgeon who had been sent to tend the prisoners reported that 'these vessels were in general infected with small-pox', alongside dysentery and putrescent fevers. In a prisoner exchange in January 1781, 740 men marched from the hulks, 530 had been released as they had joined loyalist regiments, but 800 had died. Britain was accused of inhumanity – this print shows emaciated, sick and semi-naked prisoners – but the prisoners got the same rations as the troops, and the death rate was comparable to regiments serving in the West Indies where disease killed more than bullet or bayonet.

Being sent to the hulks was also a form of punishment. When the news of the brutality towards British prisoners by the 'Swamp Fox', Colonel Marion, got out, the British commandant at Charleston, Colonel Balfour, assigned 130 American militia to the prison ships as 'hostages'.

Captive Britons in America

Americans in a British Prison

A View of the GUARD-HOUSE and SIMSBURY-MINES now called Newgate,
A Prison for the Confinement of Loyalists in Connecticut

Prisoners in America

These two very rare prints were American propaganda. The date is somewhat uncertain: it may have been the British American War of 1812 or more likely the Revolutionary War. The sentiments expressed are true for either. The British prisoners dine well with meat and wine, and are waited upon by a black servant. There is a lady, a dog and a cat to accompany them and they have been allowed to keep their smart and warm uniforms.

The American prisoners, on the other hand, are manacled in a grim cell in rags and barefoot; one seems to have died.

The Underground Prison at Connecticut (right)

British Prisoners (opposite bottom)
View of Newgate, Connecticut State Prison

These two prints show the prison in Connecticut at Newgate which was an old copper mine. Loyalists and Tories were kept in what became the first state prison in America during the war. As the print makes clear, the prisoners were kept underground in the tunnels of the mine. They were held in dark and damp conditions as all mines fill with water – their only light would be candles. In 1827 the prison was closed as the conditions in which prisoners were kept were condemned as inhuman.

Chapter Twelve

1780-1781
The Fugitive War in the South

'The enemy are penetrating this country with great rapidity,

nor do I see anything to stop their progress….

Our force is so small and in such distress that I have little to hope

and everything to fear.' General Nathanael Greene, 9 February 1780

1780

AFTER THE CAPTURE OF NEW YORK and the fall of Montreal in 1776, this was to be Britain's best year. The winter of 1779-80 was the hardest of the war – the Delaware and Hudson Rivers froze over and there were twenty-eight snow storms, some lasting three to four days. Washington, with little financial support from Congress, had difficulty in providing his men even with food. Two regiments from Connecticut stationed in New Jersey complained that they had received only 'musty bread and a little beef every other day'. A Private Martin recorded: 'We were absolutely, literally starved… I saw several men roast their own shoes and eat them.' They preferred desertion to starvation and the situation came close to violence. Even when rations were provided, they suspected that their officers were making money on the side at their expense. There were other mutinies in Pennsylvania, Rhode Island, and Charlottesville.

Washington's Continental Army had fallen from 15,000 to just 5,000. He was appalled at the indecision of Congress and its inability to get all the states to agree on united action. There was no concerted national leadership and he was even alarmed about the morale and condition of his army:

'I assure you every idea you can form of our distress will fall short of the reality. There is such a combination of circumstances to exhaust the patience of the soldiery that it begins at length to be worn out and we see in every line of the army the most serious features of mutiny and sedition.'

A major grievance was that soldiers were paid in paper money which was worth less than one percent of its face value. This led to their officers telling Congress that as wages were utterly adequate they expected to be given some of the land that they were fighting to protect. Clinton sent emissaries to infiltrate the American army to spread discontent and win recruits, but if they were caught they were hanged.

In London things were looking up. In January the news of a British fleet successfully storming the Spanish port of Omoa in the Bay of Honduras in October 1779 was a welcome fillip, especially as the value of the prizes taken was estimated at $3 million. With the stalemate in the north, Germain nagged away at Clinton to open up a southern front. In December 1778 a small and resourceful British force of 3,500 had landed in Georgia and seized the port of Savannah, with a loss of only three British dead – eighty Americans were killed and 450 captured. In September 1779 d'Estaing with a fleet of twenty-two warships and ten frigates landed 4,000 French soldiers and started to bombard Savannah. In October in a frontal assault, 3,500 French and 1,000 Americans were mown down as they advanced across a swamp. It was a valiant and successful defence by a smaller force. D'Estaing was wounded and he struck sail – another Franco-American fiasco.

Encouraged by this, Clinton left the bitter cold of New York on Boxing Day 1779 with 5,000 men and fourteen warships to retake Charleston in South Carolina, which he had spectacularly failed to do in 1776. This was the first major offensive since Saratoga. Charleston was a wealthy, civilised city – the Venice of the South – dependent upon slavery and under the domination of the 'Rice Kings'. The fat, lame, somnolent American commander, Benjamin Lincoln, believed that any attack as in 1776 would come from the sea, so he placed his main defences there. Clinton, a good field commander, decided to advance on Charleston from the north by land. In April he had received additional reinforcements – 2,500 from New York including the Black Watch and a Hessian regiment; two American regiments; and the militia from Georgia – which had increased his army to 12,500 men. Lincoln, encouraged by local citizens, decided not to abandon the city but they

withstood the fighting for only three days before the citizens changed their tune. He surrendered on 12 May – 3,600 regular soldiers were taken prisoner and 1,800 militias were paroled at a cost to the British of just seventy-six killed and 190 wounded. This British victory, the best since New York in 1776, was due to Clinton but he decided in June to return to New York leaving the southern army of 4,000 men, mainly loyalists, in the supposedly capable hands of Lord Cornwallis.

Before leaving Clinton made a devastating blunder by issuing a proclamation that all militia on parole had to swear an oath of fealty to George III; if not they would be considered rebels. This simply reinforced the determination of the militias to soldier on – it meant civil war between the loyalists and the rebels. The guerrilla leader Thomas 'Gamecock' Sumter found it easier to recruit men prepared to fight and die – he was even joined by two regiments who had taken the oath of fealty. Two of the rebel leaders were John Sevier, who was to become the first Governor of Tennessee, and Evan Shelby, the first Governor of Kentucky.

John Bull Triumphant (opposite top)
4 January 1780
James Gillray

The Spaniard is tossed by a British bull – the capture of Omoa – and a Frenchman and an Indian brave representing America cringe, fearing that they will be the next target. A Dutchman waits to see who is going to win before committing himself. Bute, North and Mansfield all seek to restrain the bull which is an odd comment since there had been very few British victories to celebrate. This is by James Gillray who in the years before 1780 had produced only a handful of prints but who was now to get into his stride and lift the whole quality of prints to works of art.

The British Tar at Omoa
1 January 1780
W H Strand

In April 1779 Charles III of Spain agreed to support France and on 16 June he declared war on Britain. He was hoping to pick up Minorca, Florida and Gibraltar. The large Spanish fleet planned to join the French and invade England. However neither fleet understood the other's signals; the Spanish arrived six weeks late; the French were hit by scurvy; and a great gale off Plymouth dispersed this latter-day Armada.

British spirits rose when its enterprising squadron in the West Indies captured the Spanish fort, Omoa, in the Bay of Honduras and seized valuable booty. The Spaniards were caught off-guard and it was reported that an English sailor who had surprised a Spanish officer in his sleep, and therefore without his sword, generously offered him own cutlass so it would be a fair fight. The Spanish flag is pulled down as the Union Jack unfurls above it.

The Bull Roasted: or the Political Cooks serving their Customers
12 February 1780

The three guilty cooks of England: George III turning the spit; Sandwich basting the bull; and North serving up delicious helpings to France, Spain and America who is asking for 'A Dish of Buttock for Congress'. The government was massively unpopular, Parliament highly critical, and petitions from all over the country were arriving demanding reform. In addition the Great Bull of Britain was being carved up for the benefit of its enemies.

The war in the south presented the British army with new challenges. John Hayes, an army physician, recorded that the British forces were brought low by illness: 'a country full of marshes and small rivers, woods and insects, and a sun so powerful in heat, with dews at night most astonishing, and to which the soldier must always be exposed are causes not to be combated with…sickness therefore was general and of the bilious kind mostly tending to putrescency… this sickness has been the reason why we are not in possession of North Carolina.' What made it worse was the uniform of the soldiers, with its wool and high stock.

The nature of the war then changed. For the rest of 1780 there were a number of skirmishes in the Carolinas, about thirty are recorded as engagements, but there were a further 176 ambushes and raids where cattle and slaves were stolen and homes burned. What remained of the Continental Army in the south west (most of the army was with Washington in New Jersey) retreated to North Carolina and the fighting was left to militia forces and loyalists reinforced by the daring cavalry troops under the command of Lieutenant-Colonel Banastre Tarleton. He was a young, energetic and ruthless adventurer who by 1778 was in command of the British Legion, a provincial unit of mounted troops. Like 'Gentleman Johnny' he had many talents: he was an occasional poet and a great philanderer – in Philadelphia he was discovered in bed with the American mistress of his senior officer and a duel almost followed.

In the southern campaigns of 1780 he was in command of light cavalry operations and that is where he earned his reputation for being the most brutal of all British commanders. On 29 May 1780 at Waxhaws Creek, his troops used only sabres and bayonets as they massacred 113 Americans and captured 203 of whom 150 were wounded, at a cost of nineteen men. The British soldiers had gone berserk: it was slaughter for the sake of slaughter, in Tarleton's own words, 'slaughter was commenced'. One British dragoon officer ruefully recorded that 'the virtue of humanity was totally forgot'. It was the worst British atrocity of the war and provoked equally savage reprisals by the militia forces.

Washington had to deploy an army against the successful marauding of the British and he was glad that his rival, the victor of Saratoga, Horatio Gates was chosen as its leader. Almost immediately on his arrival in July, misled by Sumter's optimism that thousands of militia men would rally to his flag, Gates marched south towards Camden in British-held territory. The month's march in intense heat through swampy Pine Barrens and a desert-like terrain virtually destroyed his men's capacity to fight. But encouraged by local militia leaders, and believing he had 7,000 men when there were only 3,000, on 16 August he ordered an attack on the British lines at Camden. Cornwallis had acted quickly with a forced march to Camden where he assembled an army of 2,300 men.

The battle, which lasted only an hour, was fought across a relatively narrow field only a mile wide between two swamps. The militia from Virginia were the first to crumble and panic, and failing to stop their retreat Gates himself fled the field,

The State Tinkers
10 February 1780
James Gillray

The verse at the bottom of this print clearly attributes the state of the nation to George, who is watching North chip away at the inside of the National Kettle – the Constitution – while Sandwich, responsible for the navy, and Lord George Germain, secretary of state for America, hammer holes into it from the outside. George's crown rests on a turban implying oriental despotism. Gillray hints at much more, as tinkers since the 17th century had been seen as a dangerous underclass threatening the stability of the nation, and here it is George's very ministers who are playing that part. The verse reads:

The National Kettle, which once was a good one,
For boiling of Mutton, of Beef, & of Pudding,
By fault of the Cook, was quite out of repair,
When the Tinkers were sent for, --- Behold them & Stare.

The Master he thinks, they are wonderful Clever,
And cries out in raptures, `tis done! now or never!
Yet sneering the Tinkers their old Trade pursue,
In stopping of one Hole – they're sure to make Two.

THE STATE TINKERS.

The National Kettle, which once was a good one,

For boiling of Mutton, of Beef, & of Pudding,

By the fault of the Cook, was quite out of repair,

When the Tinkers were sent for, —— Behold them & Stare.

The Master he thinks, they are wonderful Clever,

And cries out in raptures, 'tis done! now or never!

Yet sneering the Tinkers their old Trade pursue,

In stopping of one Hole —— they're sure to make Two.

Publish'd Feby. 10th 1780 by W.Humphrey No. 227 Strand.

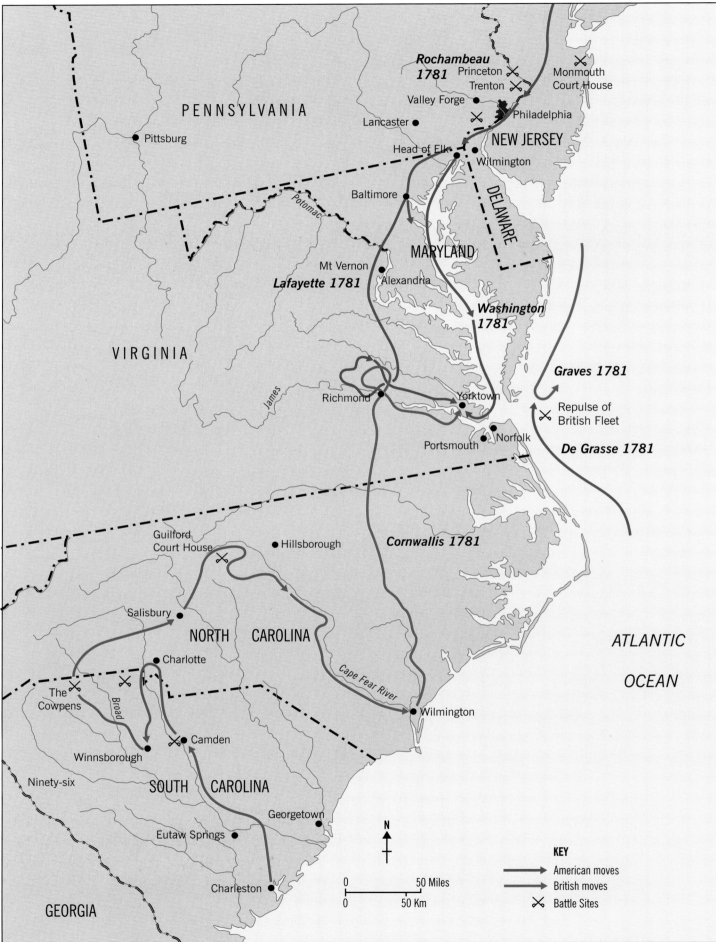

PENNSYLVANIA

Pittsburg

Rochambeau 1781

Princeton

Trenton

Monmouth
Court House

Valley Forge

Lancaster

Head of Elk

Philadelphia

NEW JERSEY

Wilmington

DELAWARE

Baltimore

MARYLAND

Potomac

Mt Vernon

Lafayette 1781

Alexandria

VIRGINIA

Washington 1781

James

Graves 1781

Richmond

Yorktown

Repulse of
British Fleet

Portsmouth

Norfolk

De Grasse 1781

ATLANTIC

OCEAN

Cornwallis 1781

Guilford
Court House

Hillsborough

Salisbury

NORTH   CAROLINA

Charlotte

Cape Fear River

The
Cowpens

Broad

Wilmington

Camden

Winnsborough

Ninety-six

SOUTH   CAROLINA

Georgetown

N

Eutaw Springs

Charleston

KEY

0   50 Miles

American moves

0   50 Km

British moves

GEORGIA

Battle Sites

ARGUS.

covering sixty miles by the evening. The British lost sixty-eight killed and 256 wounded, but the American army simply disintegrated and only 700 men rejoined the colours later in the year. Alexander Hamilton finished Gates with this comment: 'One hundred and eight miles in three days and a half; it does admirable credit to the activity of a man at his time of life. But it disgraces the general and the soldier.' Washington was glad to see him out of the way.

It was America's worst defeat since New York and it was swiftly followed two days later by another daring British triumph when Tarleton at Fishing Creek wiped out most of the militia led by Thomas Sumter. Cornwallis had rated Sumter as the most successful guerrilla leader who matched Tarleton in ruthless savagery – the dangling corpses that he left on the trees were known as 'Sumter's Fruit'.

It was the force of rebel militia led by Sumter that inflicted upon the army in the south its most savage defeat at King Mountain on 7 October. The British commander, Ferguson, was killed by the mountain men of North Carolina as they overran British troops and dozens of them fired into his corpse – 157 loyalists lay dead and 700 prisoners were taken.

In London in October North called a General Election hoping to capitalise on the British victories in the south,

Argus
15 May 1780
James Gillray

1780 was the low point for George III. All the prime ministers he had appointed since his accession twenty years earlier had let him down and in April the House of Commons had passed Dunning's famous motion, 'the influence of the crown has increased, is increasing, and ought to be diminished'. The public had come to believe that in spite of the occasional British battle success in America returning that country to colonial rule was not possible. America seen behind the throne in the feathered headdress says, 'We in America have no Crown to fight or lose'.

but that backfired as his majority was reduced to twenty-six. The country had come to realise that war was a costly affair – the national debt had doubled to more than £250 million – and new taxes would have to be levied. As a poem commented:

> Parliaments squabble and gabble,
> Ministers wonder and stare;
> Armies march backwards and forward,
> Americans stand as they were.

1781

The southern campaigns were not only the most bitter of the Revolutionary War but also the most inconclusive. There was a good deal of tit-for-tat. In December 1780, General Nathanael Greene took command of the American army in the south and he divided it between his own command and one of the most inspirational leaders on the American side, Daniel Morgan. Cornwallis despatched Tarleton to attack Morgan and they met at Hannah's Cowpens on 17 January 1781. Morgan proved the better tactician: he formed his men into three lines, placing the experienced Continental Army in the third. In the first were the militia who fired three volleys and then retired under the British attack; the troops in the second line resisted a bayonet charge but then withdrew. The British, thinking that all that was needed was a final victorious charge, met the third line of infantry 150 yards to the rear and were mown down. Morgan had told his men personally to avoid hand-to-hand fighting and to aim at the epaulettes of the British officers. The Americans at last had a victory.

Tarleton's weakness was revealed: he was a cavalry officer, a Prince Rupert and not a field officer. He lost 800 men and only managed to retreat with 300, while Morgan's losses were twelve killed and sixty wounded, but the Highlanders who had fought bravely were abandoned and they never forgave him, later savaging his memoirs: 'he led a number of brave men to destruction'.

In February Tarleton at Torrance's Tavern in North Carolina, rallying his dragoon's with the cry, 'Remember Cowpens', destroyed the North Carolina militia.

The British never succeeded in consolidating their victories as the Americans had resorted to 'hit-and-run' tactics. Nathanael Greene called it 'the fugitive war'. It was a civil war involving land and slave grab between the rebels and loyalists or, as Greene dubbed them, 'Whigs and Tories'. Many black slaves defected to the English and there were also frontiersmen who took the opportunity to attack Indians, as well as the landless poor who took every chance to kill and acquire some land. The atrocities were appalling. After the American victory of Kings Mountain many wounded British soldiers were stabbed in revenge for Tarleton's massacre at Waxhaws and in drumhead justice nine prisoners, including three loyalist officers who were regarded as traitors, were hanged. The British were no better. Major James Wemyss – 'the hanger and the burner' – hanged on a roadside gibbet a militiaman, Adam Cusack, in front of his wife and children for breaking his parole. After John Pyles' loyalists in February 1781 were hacked to death while crying for mercy, Greene's hard comment was 'it has had a very happy affect on those disaffected persons of which there are too many in this country'.

On 15 March the two forces met at Guilford Courthouse.

Greene's army was significantly larger than that of Cornwallis – his front line outnumbered the British by 800, but the redcoats were encouraged by the gallant Colonel Webster of the 23rd Regiment who rode out in front with the cry, 'Come my brave Fusiliers': he was to die in the attack. The stubborn British infantry won the day against all the odds. Greene could have won if he had deployed a regiment he held in reserve, but he lacked the spark of inspiration. It was Cornwallis, who had his horse shot from under him, who took the initiative even though damaging to his own troops, by ordering two three-pound cannons to fire grapeshot into the mass of fighting men. Both sides were mown down but it was the Americans who took flight.

This was a great victory against the odds but Cornwallis could not follow it up as his regular army only amounted to 1,400 men. It would have been humiliating to fall back to the security of Charleston where the southern campaign had started two years earlier and so he decided to march north into Virginia, the heartland of patriotic Americans, hoping to find there the elusive chance of confronting and destroying the Continental Army.

Cornwallis also advocated abandoning New York and bringing 'our whole force into Virginia; when they have a state to fight for and a successful battle may give us America.' This recognised that nothing could be achieved by battling on in the Carolinas. In writing to his close friend, General Phillips, whom he hoped would move south to join up with him he admitted quite frankly, 'I am quite tired of marching about the country in quest of adventures'. What he yearned for was a clash of arms, a meeting of two great armies in the European-style in Washington's home state.

While Cornwallis marched north, Greene marched south to Camden where he was met by Cornwallis' deputy, Lord Rawdon. The British were outnumbered but on 25 April Rawdon maintained a disciplined movement at Hobkirk's Hill

The Thunderer

James Gillray

On his return to England Tarleton, arrogant and conceited, brags to his friend, the Prince of Wales, of his success in killing Americans: 'Twenty of them, killed them…Twenty more, kill'd…thus in a day…Twenty score…that's two hundred; two hundred a day; five days a thousand'. He relished his nickname, 'Bloody Ban' and was proud of his simple credo, 'The more difficulty, the more glory'. Characteristically they both stand outside the Whirligig, a brothel, where they will be welcomed by a bare-breasted whore. Tarleton for a time lived with Perdita Robinson, the Prince of Wales' first mistress.

LONDON: Published as the ACT directs, *March* 1, 1781, and Sold by

The Budget

1 March 1781

The American war dominated Britain's public expenditure. The National Debt rose from £131 million in 1775 to £245 million in 1783. This strengthened the mood for peace. The monster in this print is the National Debt – 'the King's friend that Builds his Ships, Mans his Navy, Recruits his Army'. The taxpayers at the back protest that the war 'Strips the Country of our Finest Youths and Robs the Parents of their Children'. There is a box on the floor labelled '120,000 Guineas for America', the real cost was much higher. The army budget in 1780 was £12.2 million. The text that accompanies this print bitterly regrets going to war, 'It is not our destroying their People and their Towns will do, for we are Losers ourselves at the same Time. We were wrong at first. Had we had wise Advisers, we should have eternally traded on, fell out and made it up again, but never come to close Quarters; for by so doing we lose our own Ground.' The mood in the country had changed.

where Greene was entrenched, and they did not flinch under the American fire. His infantry were well-prepared in returning volleys of fire and they were helped by loyalist marksmen on the flanks as they advanced. The Marylanders were the first to panic and the Virginia militia just saved a complete rout.

The final victory in the south occurred on 8 September when Greene at Eutaw Springs, thirty miles north-west of Charleston, had surprised a British force. He broke through the British frontline, which was taken by surprise, but then the Americans decided to loot and pillage the British camp and, in particular, the undiluted rum. A resourceful major, John Marjoribanks, rallied his men on the right flank, launched a counterattack, and forced the Americans to flee. They were only again saved from a complete rout by a group of Maryland regulars.

This marked the end of the southern campaign. The British had won all the significant engagements in the Carolinas apart from two, but the only land they could call their own were the towns of Savannah and Charleston. Both Gates and Greene had proved poor field commanders — Greene had never effectively controlled the militia leaders, Francis Marion and Thomas Sumter, but the British victories led nowhere. Loyalist support was fragmentary and fluid since the British had failed to convince them that they would be safe under British rule after British victory; there were too many local vendettas taking place involving land and slave grab: what could be held one day could be lost tomorrow.

George Washington (above right)
1781
Paul Revere (?)
This contemporary woodcut has often been ascribed to Revere. It appeared in *The Weatherwiser's Town and County Almanack for the Year of Our Lord 1781*. Washington is not portrayed as 'a gallant warrior', although there are cannon and flags beneath the portrait. It is interesting because of its rarity.

Colonel Lord Francis Rawdon, Earl of Moira
Another disparaging French caricature, this twenty-one-year-old aristocrat was to fight throughout the war. He distinguished himself at Bunker Hill by personally leading the charge over the American defences at the top of Breeds Hill. In the close hand-to-hand fighting with bayonet and sword, he had a lucky escape as a bullet passed through his cap. General Burgoyne observed that 'Major Rawdon behaved to a charm'. In the last year of the war he led a smaller army to victory in the south at Hobkirk's Hill, checking the American General Greene's march to Charleston.

Le Lord Rawdon
arrivant dea Carolinea.

Chapter Thirteen

'The World Turned Upside Down'

Yorktown, 18 October 1781

IN THE SUMMER OF 1781 Cornwallis was impatient and also annoyed that the commission which had been promised by Lord North and the King which would have led to his appointment as the successor to Clinton as commander-in-chief remained dormant. He had nothing but contempt for Clinton's sheltering in New York, demanding more troops, supporting only two guerrilla raids and coming to the conclusion that an attack on Philadelphia was the most important thing. Against Clinton's order to consolidate the south he decided to march into Virginia on 25 April. He barely apologised to Clinton: 'it is very disagreeable to me to decide upon measures so important and of such consequence to the general conduct of the war, without an opportunity of procuring your Excellency's directions and approbations; but the delay and difficulty of conveying letters, and the impossibility of waiting for answers make it indispensably necessary.' Clinton also resented this well-connected aristocrat and confided to his ADC that Cornwallis, 'will play me false'.

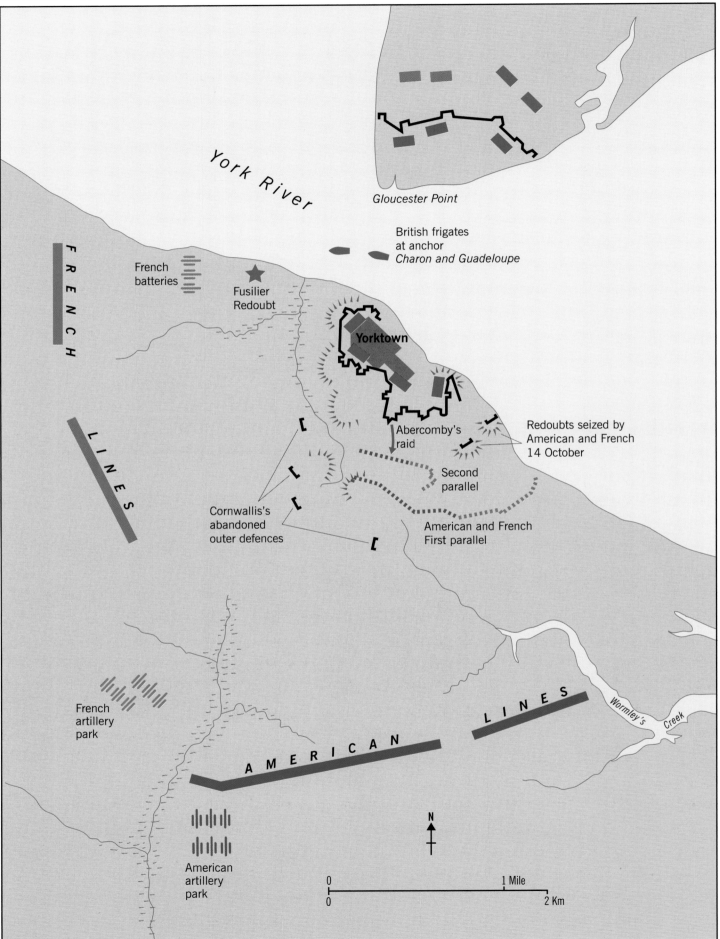

York River

Gloucester Point

British frigates
at anchor
Charon and *Guadeloupe*

French
batteries

F R E N C H

Fusilier
Redoubt

Yorktown

L I N E S

Abercomby's
raid

Redoubts seized by
American and French
14 October

Second
parallel

Cornwallis's
abandoned
outer defences

American and French
First parallel

French
artillery
park

A M E R I C A N   L I N E S

Wormley's Creek

American
artillery
park

N

0   1 Mile
0   2 Km

1. Yanky Doodle   2 Monsieur Louis Baboon.   3 Don Diego   4 Mynheer Frog.   20 Jan.1781

JACK ENGLAND Fighting the FOUR CONFEDERATES.

The decision of Cornwallis to seek a major battle in Virginia to conclude the war was an immense gamble and it rather smacked of Saratoga in reverse, only he marched north hoping to join up with the army of his old friend, General Phillips, marching south. Cornwallis was encouraged by the actions of the renegade Benedict Arnold who had made a lightning raid on Chesapeake Bay in 1780 and wintered in Portsmouth. There he was joined in March by General Phillips with 2,300 men and a French fleet, which was meant to support Lafayette's small army in Virginia, was driven off by a British fleet. Washington's army had gone through another gruelling winter and to strike into his home state seemed a brilliant strategy.

At first everything went well. Cornwallis and 1,000 men arrived on 20 May at Petersburg which had already been taken by Arnold and with 4,000 already there he then took Richmond after Lafayette abandoned it. The ever-enterprising Tarleton with 230 dragoons raided Charlottesville, the centre of Virginia's government, and the Governor, Thomas Jefferson, author of the

Jack England Fighting the Four Confederates
20 January 1781

This shows how confident Britain was in the early months of 1781. Her enemies are in disarray: Holland had 'almost forgot how to fight'. The Jolly Jack Tar – for the British fleet was enjoying a period of naval supremacy on the East Coast – thinks he could beat the lot of them as long as his British 'Land Lubbers wou'd but Pull together'.

Declaration of Independence, managed to escape with only ten minutes to spare. But Cornwallis failed to pursue Lafayette who had been reinforced by von Steuben increasing the Continental Army to 5,300. In July there was a successful skirmish with part of Lafayette's army under the command of General 'Mad' Anthony Wayne on 6 July at Green Springs where 145 Americans were killed. But once again the main American army slipped away.

British strategy over the months of May, June and July was confused and constantly changing. On 11 June Clinton

Le Général Cornwallis a Yorck le 19. 8bre 1781
a été pris prisonnier de guerre avec toute son armée
1781

The French could not resist gloating at the defeat of Cornwallis, here represented as a fox. One French soldier with a musket stops the fox, another holds his tail, and a third is about to cut it off. The ships in the background recognise that it was the French fleet which clinched the victory. No American in sight.

The State Watchman discovered by the Genius of Britain, Studying Plans for the Reduction of America
10 December 1781
James Gillray

George yet again asleep at the post. Here's Britannia's rebuke, 'Am I thus protected?' This print blames the King for Cornwallis's surrender at Yorktown on 19 October.

ships of the line'. Clinton had acted upon the advice of Admiral Graves who was to prove to be the worst admiral in the entire British fleet. Cornwallis, who had pointed out the futility of keeping a naval base in the Chesapeake that could be quite easily raided from New York, nonetheless rather surprisingly decided to accept the orders he had received and marched north, choosing Yorktown as the required base. By occupying Yorktown he surrendered the initiative and it was a singularly poor choice since there was no high ground to defend.

The American forces were divided into three: there was an army under Greene in the Carolinas which was being hammered by the British; a small force under Lafayette in the Jamestown peninsula that Cornwallis should have attacked and routed; and a third much larger force under Washington's command outside New York which was joined by Rochambeau with 3,000 well-trained and well-equipped French soldiers. In New York Clinton had 11,000 troops and Cornwallis nearly 8,000 men under arms in North Virginia. Moreover there was a large fleet in the Caribbean under Rodney and a smaller one under Graves in New York; all this added to the sense of Clinton's security. So even as late as August 1781 the balance of the advantage tipped, but only slightly in favour of the British. A crucial difference was that Washington and Rochambeau were as one, but Cornwallis and Clinton were at odds.

What was to change everything happened on 13 August when the Comte de Grasse, one of France's most experienced admirals, set sail from the West Indies with a fleet of twenty-eight warships and a number of smaller vessels which carried 3,300 French troops: their destination was Chesapeake Bay. A smaller British fleet under Hood sailed north – his commanding officer Rodney mistakenly sent too few ships – and actually reached Chesapeake before de Grasse, but finding nothing he assumed he should sail on to New York and so the Chesapeake was abandoned. In the meantime de Grasse arrived and took control of the entry to the bay.

Cornwallis was doing what he could to improve the defences of Yorktown by throwing up barriers and digging ditches, but too much was needed in too short a time. When Hood reached New York, Graves realised the threat from de Grasse and set sail with nineteen ships in an attempt to seize back control. On seeing Graves's fleet de Grasse, fearing that he would be trapped in the bay, sailed out to the open sea where the two fleets met on 13 September in what became known as the Battle of the Capes where they pounded each other for two hours. The British fleet was smaller than the French but Graves made a huge tactical error

ordered Cornwallis to send 3,000 men to New York which was threatened by Washington and Rochambeau, and accordingly Cornwallis marched south to Portsmouth, the port for embarkation. He had decided by then it was best to withdraw from Virginia and return to Charleston in South Carolina. However on 20 July he received an order from Clinton, who had accepted that the threat to New York had subsided, to 'hold a station on Chesapeake for

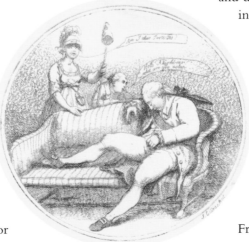

which prevented seven of his fleet engaging the French. Graves should then have followed the advice of his fellow admiral, Hood, and have immediately sailed to Chesapeake Bay, but he sailed aimlessly around for a week. De Grasse beat him to it and a smaller French fleet joined him: there were now thirty-six warships commanding Chesapeake Bay, sealing Cornwallis's fate.

Graves, whose ineptitude had led to failure in the Battle of the Capes, decided to sail back to New York – this might be excused as his natural caution and timidity, but it was close to cowardice in that he was not willing to engage the enemy. The news of de Grasse's fleet moving to Chesapeake reached Washington and Rochambeau in mid-August. They decided to abandon any attack upon New York, and march their army across the 400 miles to Chesapeake Bay. An army of 4,000 Frenchmen and 2,500 Americans set out on 19 August on the epic march. Once again Washington, as at Trenton, decided upon a bold move, but this time on a much larger scale. The risk was that he had left only 3,500 men defending the upper reaches of the Hudson, and Clinton, if he had taken the initiative, could have marched out and destroyed them.

The march south was conducted with great cunning and Washington gave the impression to Clinton's spies that he was moving the army south to Staten Island to attack New York from the south. It was not until early September that Clinton realised that Washington was actually marching to the Chesapeake. Cornwallis, unaware of Washington's tactics, still

Yorktown

1781

This Dutch print symbolically rubs in the British defeat. Four Britons in the background surrender to an American Indian at whose feet lie a broken yoke and shackles. The other Indians are directing their trade to French ports. The lean cow represents English commerce trying to graze from a few thorny branches, while a Frenchman, a Spaniard and a Dutchman relish their opportunities. An Englishman kneels in prayer while the rats gnaw away at bank notes and bills, and the British lion holding up a wounded paw howls with pain. Due credit is given to the French fleet as a British ship is sunk.

Britain's European enemies quickly realised that in America the game was up, but their hopes of getting any tangible reward for their support of America were about to be dashed.

had the opportunity to abandon Yorktown and march south as Lafayette's force would not have been able to stop him. However he expected reinforcements from Clinton and a British fleet to take on the French ships in the Chesapeake; indeed Clinton had told him that a relief force would arrive by sea on 5 October. However, neither Clinton nor Graves realised the urgency of the situation and they dillied and dallied over the repairs of ships, not leaving New York until the very day on which Cornwallis surrendered. By 28 September the now large Franco-American force of some 15,000 men and at least ninety

Reddition de l'Armée Angloises Commandée par Mylord Comte de Cornwallis aux Armées Combineés des Etats unis de l'Ameriq̃
et Glocester dans la Virginie, le 19 Octobre 1781. Il s'est trouvés dans ses deux postes 6000 hommes de troupes regleés Angloises ou Hessoises
40 Batimens dont un Vaisseau de 50 Canons qui a eté Brulé 20 Coules Bas. Ce jour a jamais memorables pour les Etats unis en ce qui̇l̃

A. Yorck Touwn   C. Armeés Angloise sortant de la place   E. Armeé Francoise   G Armeé naval de l̃
B. Glocester   D. Les Armes des ennemis poseé en Faiseeaux   F Armeé Ameriquaine   H Baye de Chesapea

...ance aux ordres des Generaux Washington et de Rochambeau a Yorck touwn
...eaux 1500 Matelots 160 Canons de tout Calibre dont 75 de Fonte & Mortiers
...nitivement leurs independances
...dres du Comte de Grace   1 Riviere d'Yorck .

A Paris chez Mondhare rue St Jean de Beauvais pres celle des Noyers.

The Surrender of the British Army at Yorktown, 18 October 1781

This French print celebrates Cornwallis's surrender. The British army in the centre is leaving Yorktown; the French army is in the front rank and the Americans are at the back. The figures at the front cannot be identified but much is made of the French fleet in Chesapeake Bay, for they made Washington's victory possible.

State Cooks, or The Downfall of the Fish Kettle
10 December 1781

The news of the surrender at Yorktown reached London at the end of November and for the first time in a print Yorktown is clearly marked on the map. George III sees only ruin before him, but North asserts that he and Germain will 'cook 'em'. Nothing could be further from North's own view which was to conclude the war in America as soon as possible. The printmaker ever anxious to put the worst case for Britain adds to the fish quota – quite wrongly – Quebec, Nova Scotia, East and West Florida.

guns started the siege of Yorktown. The town was defended by some 7,500 soldiers with 800 militia of which only 3,725 were well enough to fight, and Cornwallis had made the mistake of withdrawing from the outer defences which would have delayed the American advance by several days.

The American and French troops engaged in traditional siege warfare, establishing long trenches and having their guns in place by 9 October – the twenty-four cannons and mortars of the French smashed Cornwallis's defences. On 10 October 1,000 shells landed on Yorktown. There were two British redoubts that had to be taken and on the night of 14 October it was a French party that crept forward seizing the first after a fierce battle. There was a pre-dawn counterattack by the British on 16 October aimed at destroying the French guns. It was only partly successful for they did not have time to pour liquid metal into the gun barrels, leaving only bayonets in the gun-holes of six guns and these were quickly removed. As one last fling, Cornwallis tried to move some of his men by ship at night across the York River to Gloucester Point but that was abandoned when a storm blew up.

On 17 October at 10 o'clock in the morning a drummer appeared on the British defences and an officer waved a white flag. Washington suspended firing to receive Cornwallis's terms which he had determined would be unconditional. The British troops – some 8,000 – were to surrender with their colours folded, to give up their arms, and to be treated as prisoners of war, but the drummers were allowed to play a British march. Cornwallis was successful in being allowed to ship a small number of soldiers to New York – he chose principally deserters from the Continental Army and escaped slaves. Washington later shamefully tried to get the British to abandon their protection for these two groups.

Cornwallis sent his second in command, Brigadier O'Hara, and told him to present his sword to Rochambeau, not to Washington, signifying that it was the French not the Americans who were the decisive winners. The British troops marched out to the tune of 'The World turned upside down' before they contemptuously threw down their rifles. One of the verses ran:

> *If ponies rode men and if grass ate the cows*
> *And cats could be chased into holes by the mouse,*
> *If summer were spring and t'other way round,*
> *Then all the world would be upside down.*

In the 18th century surrender was an art form. To the amazement and annoyance of the Americans, the French victors treated the British officers right royally and Rochambeau even lent Cornwallis £10,000 to pay his men.

Yorktown was a French victory. There were 25,000 French soldiers and sailors who outnumbered the 5,000 American troops by 5:1. The strategy was determined by the decision of de Grasse

Lord North on the Stool of Repentance
March 1782
Sherwin

Lord North, fat and ungainly, sits on a close stool reading the leading Opposition paper *The London Courant*. He had added to his unpopularity with proposed taxes on salt, soap and places of entertainment – all needed to pay for the war. However he was tired of office and simply could not take any more and so on 20 March he resigned. Some prints even hinted that he should be impeached.

For taxing of Salt, Tobacco and Soap,
Some say that Lord North is deserving a Rope.

to ignore New York and control the Chesapeake Bay – he was helped by the faltering timidity of Admiral Graves. Washington and Rochambeau, north of New York, realised that de Grasse's move created an enormous opportunity and they quickly decided on the 400-mile march to the Chesapeake. This was undoubtedly the most decisive and inspired decision of Washington's generalship. It was even more daring and risky than Trenton and Princeton for he had to divide his army leaving a small part in the north which was vulnerable to an attack by Clinton. But here, again, Washington's judgement was spot-on for he knew Clinton was too uncertain, too diffident, too insecure, and too timid to strike in the north when Cornwallis was exposed in the south. Without the French though, the British would not have suffered the knock-out blow at Yorktown.

Chapter Fourteen

1782 – The Piss of Peace

THE NEWS OF THE SURRENDER reached London on 25 November 1781. Lord North exclaimed, 'It is all over', but George III had a more measured judgement:

'I have no doubt when men are a little recovered of the shock felt by bad news, and feel that if we recede no one can tell to what a degree the consequence of this country will be diminished, that they will find the necessity of carrying on the war, though the mode of it may require alteration.'

This optimism may not have been such a misjudgement for Washington had wanted to press on and take back Savannah and Charleston but he had to return to New York as de Grasse decided within a fortnight to move on to an even more important sphere of engagement – the West Indies. However, the effect of the Yorktown debacle was to move the balance in London decisively in favour of the peace party which had been steadily gathering strength, since the war party could not deliver success or victory.

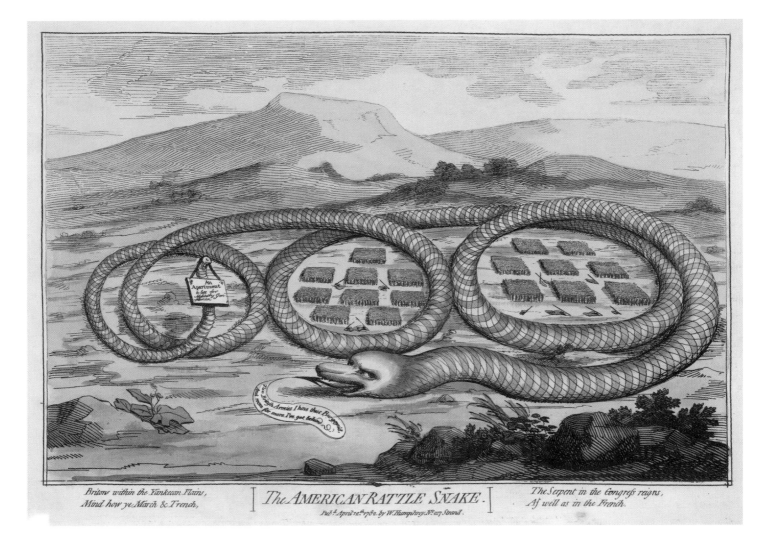

Britons within the Yankeean Plains,
Mind how ye March & Trench,

The AMERICAN RATTLE SNAKE.

Pub.d April 12.th 1782. by W.Humphrey. N.o 227 Strand.

The Serpent in the Congress reigns,
As well as in the French.

The American Rattlesnake
12 April 1782
James Gillray

This dramatic and brilliant print uses the rattlesnake as the symbol of a successful America that has caught in its coils two British armies – Burgoyne's and Cornwallis's – and its deadly rattle is waiting for the third. This is an expression of the confidence of a victor, warning-off all those who still hoped that Britain would fight on.

Britons within the Yankeean Plains,
Mind how ye March & Trench,
The Serpent in the Congress reigns,
As well as in the French.

Germain's first reaction was to devise a plan to continue the war based upon the secure possessions of New York, Charleston and Savannah with an army of over 28,000 men. This was in vain. In November the royal address was attacked in both Houses and on 8 December the Cabinet decided to send no more troops to America. On 7 February 1782 the government's majority was twenty-two falling lower on 22 February; and on 27 February it was defeated when a motion was carried:

That the further prosecution of offensive warfare on the continent of North America for the purpose of reducing the revolted colonies to obedience by force, will be the means of weakening the efforts of this country against her European enemies.

The opposition MPs were always a minority and by themselves could never have carried this motion. It was the Knights of the Shires, the independent country members who rarely spoke in debates as loyal supporters of King George, who decided that it was time to vote otherwise or the war would drift on unsuccessfully and then taxes would have to rise. So, ironically just as taxation started the war, it also helped to end it.

Clinton was replaced by Sir Guy Carleton; Germain resigned and received the viscouncy he had asked for; and on 20 March North, to the chagrin and anger of the King, announced to the House of Commons that he had resigned – George III did not even thank him for his services. No more troops were sent to America and in July 1782 the British army evacuated Savannah, in December Charleston, and in November 1783 New York.

A coalition under the aged Rockingham set about the peace negotiations which were led by Shelburne with Charles James Fox firing from the sidelines. Following Rockingham's

BRITANIA'S ASSASSINATION.
or ____ The Republicans Amusement.

death in June, Shelburne became prime minister until he was ousted by the unnatural coalition of Fox and North in March 1783. The peace terms were a victory won by Shelburne.

In the aftermath of Yorktown Franklin had wanted Canada to be added to the thirteen states, but British luck began to change and in April 1782 Rodney defeated and captured de Grasse at the Battle of the Saints in the Caribbean; a Franco-Spanish invasion of Jamaica was abandoned; and Gibraltar triumphantly resisted a siege. Shelburne divided the coalition by ignoring France and Spain and concluded a separate treaty with America which was announced on 30 November 1782 without even telling the French foreign minister, Vergennes.

WHO WERE THE WINNERS AND THE LOSERS?

America's independence was recognised and her territories extended well beyond the Proclamation Line of 1763 up to the Great Lakes and into the heart of the American continent. George III at last recognised the inevitable:

'We meant well to the Americans – just to provide them with a few bloody noses and then to make laws for the happiness of both countries. But lack of discipline got into the Army, lack of skill and energy into the Navy, and lack of unity at home. We lost America.'

Britania's Assassination
10 May 1782
James Gillray

The supporters of the new government that replaced North are seen to be assaulting Britannia – Dunning, Fox, Richmond and Burke are led by John Wilkes. Only the two lawyers, Mansfield and Thurlow, try to restrain them. Meanwhile an American Indian runs off with Britannia's head and France, Spain and Holland slip away grabbing what they can. *The Morning Chronicle* believed that this print was the most important for years as it did not flinch from berating an entire ministry. This is Gillray associating the Whigs with republicanism.

But America paid a heavy price. One out of every 200 Americans had died; the economy had virtually collapsed under the trade embargoes; and disruption of the sowing and harvesting of crops made food scarce. It had also tasted in the south the bitter fruit of a civil war.

Britain had been humiliated having lost a colony of over two and a half million people, but it did learn some lessons. In 1791 the Canada Act recognised that decentralised administration was necessary and it gave to Canada legislative autonomy – the offer of the Carlisle Commission in 1778. The British army, which had won far more victories than the American, was hardened by the experience and professionally prepared for the French Revolutionary and Napoleonic Wars.

The French gained St Lucia but were to lose it again by 1815. Their hopes of regaining a position in North America as the new country's European ally were rebuffed: they could not even get favourable trading terms. Vergennes was shocked by the duplicity of the British doing a deal behind his back and he was even more astonished at the British terms: 'Their concessions exceeded all that I thought possible. The English buy peace rather than make it.' France received no contribution from America to help with its war debts which added to the financial and political crisis that was to hurl the country towards revolution.

There were two other clear losers – the Native Indian tribes and the loyalists. The Oneida, Mohican and Catawba tribes lost virtually all their lands. By 1830 the Oneida tribe was reduced from six million acres to thirty-two; the Mohicans were restricted to six square miles and then moved to Wisconsin. The Catawba reservation was down to one square mile in South Carolina. The Sons of Liberty knew what they were about – another generation would have called this ethnic cleansing.

Under the peace treaty it was left to the states to treat loyalists fairly. There were a lot of them: 100,000 had been prepared to serve in the militias or as regular soldiers, and many came from former colonial establishments – people who had a significant stake and role in their communities. Forty thousand lost their properties and even if they took the Oath of Allegiance to the United States, they were denied public office or a career in the professions. It was not surprising then that some 80,000-100,000 left their homes to go to Canada and the West Indies, and 8,000 chose Britain. In three weeks in May 1783, 7,556 people applied for passage from New York alone to go to Canada. What was America's loss was Canada's gain, for the 40,000 who went there were in effect Canada's founding fathers. It is indeed ironic that the strength they gave to Canada prevented its annexation by America.

The loyalists made claims for compensation amounting to £10 million and Britain finally settled for £3 million. Many felt that George III had let them down:

Ah! George – that name provokes my keenest rage,
Did he not swear, and promise, and engage
His Loyal sons to nurture and defend,
To be their God, their father and their friend –
Yet basely quits us on a hostile coast,
And leaves us wretched where we need him most;
His is the part to promise and deceive,
By him we wander and by him we grieve;
Since the first day that these dissentions grew,

When Gage to Boston brought this blackguard crew,
From place to place we urge our vagrant flight
To follow still this vapour of the night,
From town to town have run our various race,
And acted all that's mean and all that's base –
Yes – from that day until this hour we roam,
Vagrants forever from our native home.

George III was a loser – he even drafted an abdication speech and prepared to go into exile to his hereditary state of Hanover. Catherine the Great of Russia was blunter: 'Rather than sign the separation of thirteen provinces like my brother George, I would have shot myself.' For the rest of his reign he felt a great sense of guilt that he had personally let down his country and his empire. 'I never lay my head on my last pillow in peace and quiet so long as I remember the loss of my American colonies.' But he never accepted that he had played a major role in that loss for he always saw himself as supporting his ministers in their duty to hold the empire together.

Rodney Introducing de Grasse (opposite top)
April 1782
James Gillray

Rodney beat the French fleet under the command of de Grasse at the Battle of the Saints in April 1782 and that made him a popular hero. Here he presents de Grasse, the one Frenchman who had secured the British defeat at Yorktown just six months earlier, to George III – as a trophy. North had recalled Rodney as Fox wanted to replace him with Admiral Pigot – Fox is standing to the left of the throne. Pigot had lost so much to Fox playing Pharo at Brooks' that he was sent out to re-establish his career and possibly earn his fortune in the West Indies. This victory improved Britain's hand in the diplomatic negotiations over the Peace Treaty – Shelburne was no longer on the back-foot and he was able to isolate America and ignore France. The successful defence of Gibraltar against a Franco-Spanish attack meant no concessions to Spain either.

The Horros of War a Vision or
A Scene in the Tragedy of Rich[d] 3
20 August 1782
Sharpe

This is a reflection on the defeat of Britain. Britannia blames Corruption, shown as a satyr who is saying whilst looking at North that its business is nearly over. North is angry that 'disgrace and public detestation' are his lot. An American Indian with a sword through her breast, standing on a cloud with four dead children and the grisly implements of war, including a scalping knife, reproaches Germain on the couch and Sandwich in the corner for pressing on with an inhuman war. The vision of the horrors of war alarms Germain just as Richard III was visited by a vision before Bosworth.

The Habeas Corpus, or The Wild Geese flying away with Fox to America

The Habeas Corpus, or The Wild Geese flying away with Fox to America
27 August 1782

In Rockingham's government earlier in the year, Fox and Shelburne fell out over the American peace negotiations. Fox favoured the immediate recognition of American independence and Shelburne wanted to hold back to strengthen his negotiating arm with France. On Rockingham's death in July, Fox resigned and returned to opposition where he espoused the American cause even more strongly. The geese are pulling him away from Westminster to the 'dear Independent Congress' and the leading swan asserts, 'To America he shall go for his heart is there'.

The American Rattlesnake presenting Monsieur his Ally a Dish of Frogs.

The American Rattlesnake presenting Monsieur his Ally a Dish of Frogs
8 November 1782

The rattlesnake, now an emblem of America, gives a basket of frogs as a gift to its ally, to allay France's suspicion that America was negotiating a separate peace with Britain behind their backs. That is just what Richard Oswald, the British representative, was doing with the American commissioners and a preliminary treaty was signed on 30 November, without France being told. Benjamin Franklin, the master of the double-bluff, did not tell the French as he still hoped to borrow a substantial sum from them for his new country. There is a spirited verse accompanying the print:

O Britons be wise
And part these Allies
Or drive them both into the Bogs;
I think it is Fit
They both should be submit
To Old England, or live upon Frogs.

The RECONCILIATION between BRITANIA and her daughter AMERICA.

The Reconciliation between Britannia and her daughter America

Britannia wants to kiss America who addresses her as 'Mama'. Fox, not liking the pulling power of France and Spain, tells Admiral Keppel to give them both a spank. This gives far too much credit to Fox as it was Shelburne who wanted to divide America from its European allies by delaying immediate recognition of America's independence. But this is how it turned out – France and Spain were sidelined and the successful coalition broken apart by astute British diplomacy.

The BELLIGERANT PLENIPO'S

AMERICA TRIUMPHANT and BRITANNIA in DISTRESS

The Belligerant Plenipo's
December 1782
Colley

Peace negotiations had been going on between Britain and America since the spring and on 30 November preliminary articles between England and America were signed in Paris. America had won – here she stands smiling on the right holding half of George's crown and saying, 'I have got all I wanted'. The French are fed-up at getting nothing and losing an arm which lies at George's feet; the Dutch, in patched clothes reflecting their economic hardship, have lost a foot; Spain angrily demands Gibraltar in lieu of its lost leg; while above them all Ireland emphasises her own constitutional freedom. George crossly declares, 'I gave them independence'.

America Triumphant and Britannia in Distress
1782
Weatherwise Almanac

This was the frontispiece to the almanac. America, under the Stars and Stripes and holding an olive branch, encourages the fleets of the world to come to New York and trade with the new independent country. Fame with her bugle spreads the good news while Britannia, with a broken spear and the British flag toppling into the sea, weeps for her lost trade. This is really rubbing Britain's nose in it, for the war had as its origins the desire of the mother country to control the trade of her offspring to her own advantage.

Charles James Fox would not let him escape the responsibility:

'There was one grand domestic evil, from which all our other evils, foreign and domestic, had sprung. To the influence of the Crown we must attribute the loss of the army in Virginia; to the influence of the Crown we must attribute the loss of the thirteen provinces in America; for it was the influence of the Crown in the two Houses of Parliament, that enabled His Majesty's ministers to persevere against the voice of reason, the voice of truth, the voice of the people. This was the grandparent spring from which all our misfortunes flowed.'

It is not surprising that George detested Fox, but he had his revenge in 1783 by dismissing the coalition government that Fox dominated.

George Washington was the clear winner for without his cool, steady leadership the revolution would have collapsed. Congress was an ineffectual debating chamber that had little power and no money – the soldiers had to be paid with IOUs. His great achievement was to hold the Continental Army together and avoid its annihilation in any major battle – that was the sure guarantee that the revolution would succeed. This was not glorious, but effective and eventually victorious. After the war some of his senior officers wanted him to become a king – a military despot – but he bluntly rejected their ideas. His greatest achievements were yet to come. He agreed to the demobilisation of the army and set out in 1783 the path that America should follow if it were to become a great country:

Blessed are the PEACE MAKERS

'First an indissoluble union of the States under one federal head. Secondly a sacred regard to public justice (that is the payment of debts). Thirdly the adoption of a proper peace establishment (that is an army and a navy). Fourthly the prevalence of that specific and friendly disposition among the people of the union, which will influence them to forget their local prejudices and policies; to make those mutual concessions, which are requisite to the general prosperity; and in some instances, to sacrifice their individual advantages to the interest of the community.'

This is not high flown rhetoric but it is the cool, solid assessment of what the thirteen states had to do to become a great country. Two years later, he wrote to Henry Knox that without a serious federal government, 'we are no more than a rope of sand and shall as easily be broken'. This was his blueprint and over the following three years it inspired the conservative elite in the leading states to fashion and to forge the constitution of America which has survived to this day. George Washington deserves his heroic position.

There is an interesting postscript for the most unlikely winner of the war was the English language. During the peace negotiations in Paris a Frenchmen predicted that the thirteen colonies would become 'the greatest empire in the world'. One of the American delegates quickly responded with: 'Yes, Sir, and they will all speak English, every one of 'em.'

Blessed are the Peacemakers
24 February 1783

In the ultimate humiliation Spain and France lead George by a halter through a gateway of spears from which the British lion, crown and unicorn are falling. He is followed by Lord Shelburne, the smug peace negotiator and prime minister since July 1782. They are scourged by America with a lash of thirteen tails who is leading a disconsolate Dutchman. On 21 February the Commons rejected Shelburne's peace terms, barely any members having a good word to say for him, and the next day George wrote, 'I am sorry it has been my lot to reign in the most profligate Age and when the most unatural [sic] coalition seems to have taken place, which can but add confusion and distraction among a too much divided Nation.' On the very day this print appeared Shelburne resigned.

The General P---s, or Peace (opposite)
19 January 1783

The separate peace terms agreed between Britain, France and Spain were to be signed at Versailles on 20 January 1783 shortly after this print was published. Differences had to be buried, though France cannot resist a waspish retort: 'We have wrangled you out of America', and the Americans, represented by an Indian: 'A free and independent p---'. The English have to be content with: 'I call this an honourable p....'.

The General P—s, or Peace.

The Savages Let loose, or The Cruel Fate of the Loyalists
March 1783

The Savages Let loose, or The Cruel Fate of the Loyalists
March 1783
Some loyalists are hanged and two are being axed and scalped by
Indians. Having lost, the loyalists got a poor deal in the peace
negotiations. They did not suffer at the hands of the Indians, but
rather at the hands of their fellow Americans who were glad to
enforce the penal legislation and to confiscate their property.
There was much resentment and the luckier ones fled to Canada
where George III supported schemes to provide them with land.

The phrase beneath the print points up their desperate
situation. They felt betrayed and many in England were
embarrassed at their treatment. A contemporary squib ran:

T'is an honour to serve the bravest of nations
And to be left to be hanged in their capitulations.

But as with all conflicts: to the victor the spoils.

Mrs General Washington, Bestowing thirteen Stripes on Britania.

The *Ramblers* magazine carried a scurrilous report that Washington was really a woman. It was absurd but a reminder that Britain could not even beat a woman.

America Presenting at the Altar of Liberty Medallions of her Illustrious Sons
1783

This British engraving which would have been done from a copperplate is printed on cotton for sale in America. It could have been used as a cloth, or a cushion cover or even a curtain. As soon as the war was over British merchants were keen to re-establish trading links – and imagined nothing better than a romantic and idealised portrayal of the victor, George Washington, crowned by Fame and escorted by Victory with her foot on a British shield, pointing to the figure of America (still a woman though no longer defenceless) who kneels before Liberty with the medallions of the heroes of the revolution.

Intelligence on the Peace (opposite)
October 1783
Robert Dighton

The Gazette of 6-9 September carried the news that peace had been signed and it was proclaimed on 6 October. The way in which the news was received in London was a favourite theme for Robert Dighton – in one of his prints a barber is so astonished he cuts the man he is shaving. In this case, a cobbler neglects his business to pass on the news to a motley crew: one sticks out his tongue; a small chimney sweep is absorbed; the man helping to fill the lamps spills the oil on the ground; while a baker with a basket and a barber with a long box stop to listen. Peace – so what!

The Franklin Seal
1783
Louis-Alexandre La Rochefoucauld-d'Enville from *Constitutions des Treize Etats-Unis de l'Amériqué*, Philadelphie, Paris

This is the first appearance of the seal which Benjamin Franklin helped to design. This book was published with Franklin's encouragement and at his expense. It contained the constitution of the original thirteen states, the Declaration of Independence, the Articles of Confederation and agreements of trade and friendship with France, the Netherlands, and Sweden. While Franklin was the US ambassador to the French court he suggested to La Rochefoucauld-d'Enville that he should translate the English version of the constitution which had been published in Philadelphia in 1781. Several of the concepts were difficult to translate – the 'pursuit of happiness' and the political settlement that had been made in America had little effect upon the Ancien Regime which was entering its last fatal period. The title page of the book bore for the first time the newly-designed seal of the United States.

Peace!Peace!erye Monsieur,before Hood again calls:
Spain Welcomes the sound,dreading Eliotts hot Balls:
Return but my Gelt,Holland roars out in fear,
I too,will make peace;Indeed!will you Myneer?

PROCLAMATION
of
PEACE

Aye Sink me you shall, and for you, Miss revolt,
The time may yet come,to repent of your fault.

Proclamation of Peace
21 October 1783

Peace was signed on 2/3 September and proclaimed in London on 6 October – but was not made with Holland until 1784. The Frenchman who got nothing consoles the Spaniard for failing to seize Gibraltar, and a determined burly English sailor threatens the Dutchman that if he does not make peace then they will lose their spice trade in the Far East. The American Indian with tomahawk, Cap of Liberty and striped American flag declares that America will control its own destiny indifferent to all the European powers, 'I have got my Liberty, and the Devil scalp you all'. The last two lines of the verse read:

Aye Sink me you shall, and for you, Miss revolt,
The time may yet come, to repent of your fault.

It reflects a view popular at the time that one day Fate would catch-up with the rebellious colonies.

Plate 4 from 'America, a Prophecy' (opposite)
1793
William Blake

Blake, no lover of regal power, in his poem "America, a Prophecy" assigns much of the blame for the loss of the American colonies to George, 'The Guardian Prince of Albion'. The verse that precedes this illustration starts:

On his cliffs stood Albion's wrathful Prince,
A dragon form, clashing his scales: at midnight he arose
And flam'd red meteors round the land of Albion beneath;
His voice, his locks, his awful shoulders, and his glowing eyes
Appear to the Americans upon the cloudy night.

Various aspects of George's power are represented here: the dragon, 'The Guardian Prince of Albion', throwing down thunderbolts; the white bearded figure 'Albion's Angel' with tablets of law and the sceptre; the crouching figure who holds his hands over his head – a common gesture for a clouded mind – might allude to George's madness. Later in the poem Blake describes the physical symptoms of George's insanity.

Appear to the Americans upon the cloudy night.

Solemn heave the Atlantic waves between the gloomy nations,
Swelling, belching from its deeps red clouds & raging fires.
Albion is sick. America faints! enrag'd the Zenith grew.
As human blood shooting its veins all round the orbed heaven
Red rose the clouds from the Atlantic in vast wheels of blood
And in the red clouds rose a Wonder o'er the Atlantic sea;
Intense! naked! a Human fire fierce glowing, as the wedge
Of iron heated in the furnace; his terrible limbs were fire
With myriads of cloudy terrors banners dark & towers
Surrounded; heat but not light went thro' the murky atmos-
                                                        -phere

The King of England looking westward trembles at the vision

(VISION

King George

THE GREATEST IRONY of the American Revolution was that when George Washington assumed the role of president in 1787, he was given greater personal powers than were ever enjoyed by George III. He could appoint not only ministers but ambassadors, consuls, administrative officers and Supreme Court judges, and as commander-in-chief he could send his country to war, make treaties and conduct his own foreign policy independent of Congress.

In 1776 it suited the rebels to demonise George III as a tyrant. In earlier years the target for attack had been the British Parliament and insensitive British ministers, but it was necessary to have a more personal target to motivate the patriotism of the foot soldiers of the revolution. The United States had to be seen to emerge as a nation by confronting and defeating a foreign despot.

The consequence of the Revolutionary War was that the people of America swapped a hereditary monarchy with limited powers for an elective monarchy which had much wider powers. The revolutionaries who had hoped for some wider distribution of power in the new American state were disappointed. Hannah Griffiths, a Quaker from Pennsylvania, in 1785 said it in verse:

George Washington
Washington to John Adams:
'Sir, you have given yourselves a King under the title of President.'

The glorious fourth – again appears
The day of days – and the year of years
The sum of sad disasters.
When all the mighty gains we see
With all their boasted liberty
Is only change of masters.

The constitution agreed in September 1787 was shaped by a Conservative elite – planters, farmers, merchants, lawyers, bankers and businessmen – the radicals and revolutionaries were simply excluded. The President, the Senate, the House of Representatives and the Supreme Court created a centralised government whose powers far exceeded the British colonial system that it had overthrown. The popular uprising known as Shay's Rebellion was ruthlessly suppressed in 1786 and in 1794 when disgruntled Pennsylvanians objected to an excise duty on whisky, which was virtually indistinguishable from the levies that Britain had imposed thirty years earlier, Washington ordered 15,000 troops to quell the revolt. Tom Paine, the hero of 1776 and who had coined the phrase 'The United States of America', on visiting again at the end of Washington's second term, wondered 'whether you have abandoned good principles, or whether you ever had any'.

Washington had become the first president in April 1789. He was partially deaf and almost toothless, but he knew that he was needed to bind the country together. One of his first acts was to designate 26 November as a day of Thanksgiving.

The founders of the constitution had made the executive head, the president, also the ceremonial head of the country. Washington revelled in this and during the debate on what title

should be used to show respect he secretly favoured the style of 'High Mightiness'. He was one of the wealthiest men in America – Robert Morris, the wealthy New York banker, referred to him as 'America's first Millionaire'. He had all the trappings of a monarch: six white horses drew his canary-coloured carriage and when he ceremonially visited New York a choir on a ship alongside praised him in verses sung to the tune of 'God Save the King'. His wife, Martha, held court in her salon on Friday evenings, just as Queen Charlotte did in her drawing room in London, and her husband remained aloof, not shaking hands with anyone. Many appreciated these

George III
On hearing that Washington was not going to stand again as president for a third term, he generously acknowledged that he was 'the most distinguished character of the age'.

trappings of royalty – the African-born Phyllis Wheatley put it neatly in verse:

> A crown, a mansion, and a throne that shine,
> With gold unfading, Washington! Be thine.

BOOKS FOR FURTHER READING

Bicheno, Hugh, *Rebels and Redcoats*, Harper Collins, 2003

Bingham, Clarence, *Paul Revere's Engraving*, Athenaeum, 1969

Black, Jeremy, *War for America*, Sutton Publishing, 1991

Black, Jeremy, *George III: America's Last King*, Yale University Press, 2006

Brooke, John, *King George III*, Constable, 1972

Burns, Eric, *Virtue, Value and Vanity*, Arcade Publishing, 2007

Cash, Arthur H, *John Wilkes: The Scandalous Father of Civil Liberty*, Yale University Press, 2006

Dolmetsch, Joan, *Rebellion and Reconciliation*, University Press of Virginia, 1976

Fenn, Elizabeth, *Pox Americana: The Great Smallpox Epidemic 1775-82*, Hill and Wang, 2001

Harvey, Robert, *A Few Bloody Noses*, John Murray, 2001

Hibbert, Christopher, *George III: A Personal History*, Viking, 1998

Jones, Michael Wyn, *The Cartoon History of the American Revolution*, London Editions, 1977

McCullough, David, *1776*, Simon and Schuster, 2005

Murrell, William, *A History of American Graphic Humour*, Cooper Square Press, New York, 1933

National Maritime Museum, *1776*, Catalogue for an exhibition held in 1976

Rienner, Lynne, *Resistance, Politics and the American Struggle for Independence*, Lynne Rienner Publishers 1986

Schlessinger, Arthur, *Prelude to Independence*, Alfred H Knopf, 1958

Simms, Brendan, *Three Victories and a Defeat*, Allen Lane, Penguin Books, 2007

Urban, Mark, *Fusiliers, Eight Years with the Redcoats in America*, Faber, 2007

Weintraub, Stanley, *Iron Tears, Rebellion in America*, Simon & Schuster, 2005

Wright, Esmond, *Fabric of Freedom*, Macmillan, 1961

LIST OF CHARACTERS

ADAMS, John, 1735-1826 Always slightly jealous of Washington. A Peace Commissioner in France and ambassador in London. A leading federalist and was America's second president.

ADAMS, Samuel, 1722-1803 A failure in business but a brilliant success as an urban terrorist. Inveterate plotter, fanning flames of mayhem and master of 'rent-a-mob'. Founded 'Sons of Liberty' and signed the Declaration of Independence. Distrusted and overlooked.

ANDRÉ, Major John, 1750-1780 Served as an officer at the battles of Brandywine, Paoli, Germantown and Monmouth. ADC to Howe in 1778 and appointed Adjutant-General by Clinton in October 1779. Responsible for running spies – the MI6 of the day. A long and secret correspondence with Benedict Arnold, who wanted to defect, led to a clandestine meeting in rebel-held territory in September 1780. Failing to get back to the English boat he had to spend a day disguised in civilian clothes; that was his death-knell as it made him a spy for which he was to hang.

ARNOLD, Benedict, 1741-1801 A brilliant field commander – popular with his troops. Outstanding in the march to Quebec and Saratoga. Defected to the British in 1780 and led daring raids in Chesapeake Bay. Not really welcomed in Britain after the war, dying there poor and almost forgotten.

BRANT, Colonel Joseph, 1742-1807 The Mohawk British army officer who robustly resisted Washington's ethnic cleansing of Indian tribes. Visited London twice and was awarded land concessions from the British Government for his people in Canada.

BURGOYNE, John, 1722-1792 'Gentleman Johnny' responsible for Britain's first devastating defeat at Saratoga. Returned to London to defend his reputation and serve the Whigs.

CARLETON, General Sir Guy, 1724-1808 Disliked by Germain but one of the most successful British generals. Governor in Canada until 1778, he replaced Clinton in 1782 and fought for better treatment of loyalists, blacks and Indian tribes.

CHATHAM, William Pitt the Elder, 1708-1778 Led Britain to victory in the Seven Years War; consolidated India and Canada as the heart of the British Empire. Opposed the war in America, but baulked at Independence. Charismatic and gouty, eloquent and at times mad.

CLINTON, Sir Henry, 1738-1795 Commander-in-Chief from 1778, was a good field commander – Brooklyn Heights and the capture of Charleston – but a hopeless war leader. Indecisive, insecure, sensitive to criticism and jealous of Cornwallis, he yearned to go home – his yearnings should have been met.

CORNWALLIS, Earl, 1738-1805 Given command of the South in 1778, securing British victories at Camden and Guilford Courthouse. Holding a dormant commission to replace Clinton he treated his commanding officer with disdain and disrespect. His march north into Virginia that led to the humiliation of his surrender at Yorktown was his policy and he must share the blame. Over-rated but well-connected he went onto greater things: Governor General in India and suppressor of the Irish rebellion of 1798.

D'ESTAING, Comte, 1725-1794 French admiral who failed to help the Americans at Newport, Rhode Island and at Savannah. Held low views of his allies and being wounded returned to France but during the Revolution he was guillotined after gallantly supporting Marie Antoinette.

DE LAFAYETTE, Marquis, 1752-1834 An aristocrat on the loose. Doted on by Washington and was immediately promoted to Major General. Disappointed not to be Commander-in-Chief of the French troops. Given a minor role at Yorktown. Managed to survive the French Revolution.

FOX, Charles James, 1749-1806 The first Leader of the Opposition. Ignoring unpopularity he consistently opposed the War. He flayed the government in the House of Commons.

FRANKLIN, Benjamin 1706-1790 Printer, author, inventor, diplomat – the intellectual of the Revolutionaries. Never one to miss turning a dishonest penny or a pretty girl.

GAGE, Thomas, 1720-1787 Having served in the Seven Years War became in 1763 Commander-in-Chief for North America. He was a stolid loyalist with little imagination or foresight. In 1773 on a visit to London when he told George III that resolute action was necessary – he was made the Governor of Massachusetts. His advance on Lexington and Concord started the War. He was sacked for bungling Bunker Hill.

GATES, Horatio, 1728-1800 British soldier with a chip on his shoulder. Lucky to be in command at Saratoga but his luck ran out at Camden.

GERMAIN, Lord George Sackville, 1716-1785 Dubbed the 'Coward of Minden' for his conduct in the Seven Years War, but he demanded a court martial that cleared him. Secretary of State for the American Colonies from November 1775, he was in charge of the war 3,000 miles away. Cold and aloof his optimism about British success and American inadequacy was consistently wrong. His orders confused his generals.

GREENE, Nathanael, 1742-1786 Helped Washington to create the Continental Army at Valley Forge. A poor field commander but Washington's most favoured general.

De GRASSE, Rear Admiral Comte, 1722-1788 France's most experienced admiral. His fleet which sailed from the West Indies to Chesapeake Bay in September 1781 clinched victory for the Americans by sealing off the retreat of Cornwallis's army. Grasse deserves the gold medal of the war.

HANCOCK, John, 1737-1793 Wealthy Boston merchant whose fortune came from the smuggling of rum and wine. When one of his ships was seized by Customs in 1768 he was so popular that a mob burnt the Customs boat. A close ally of Sam Adams, in 1774 was elected as the President of the first Constitutional Congress that passed the Declaration of Independence. His generous philanthropy in Boston made him popular but he was a touch too flashy for a major national figure.

HOWE, General William 1729-1814 Appointed Commander-in-Chief following Gage's recall. Failed to hold Boston. Although he captured New York he did not pursue Washington's army and destroy it. His role as a Peace Commissioner muddled his mission. He failed to meet up with Burgoyne's army, preferring to capture the strategically important Philadelphia. Replaced as C-in-C in 1778 by Henry Clinton.

HOWE, Lord 1726-1799 An experienced sailor who was Commander-in-Chief of the Navy from 1776-1778 which was the least successful part of a long naval career. The blockade of ports to prevent French support was ineffective and his fleet was largely used to ferry around British soldiers: 256 ships committed to taking the troops to Philadelphia. He returned to London in 1778, appointed to full Admiral, and found fame in beating the French in 1796 on the Glorious 1st June.

JEFFERSON, Thomas, 1743-1826 Drafted the Declaration of Independence. His 'inalienable rights' did not extend to negro slaves, one of whom bore him several children. Third President of the USA, 1801-1809.

MORGAN, Brigadier Daniel, 1736-1802 His parents were Welsh. He served as a British soldier in the Seven Years War and got 500 lashes for striking down an officer. Joined the rebel army in 1765, fighting well at Saratoga, and gave America its greatest victory at Cowpens in January 1781.

PAINE, Thomas, 1737-1809 Itinerant revolutionary. His *Common Sense* pamphlet was America's first bestseller. First to coin the phrase 'The United States of America'. Later too revolutionary for the Sons of Liberty and refused American citizenship.

REVERE, Paul, 1734-1818 A silversmith, a copperplate engraver, a dentist and a trusted express rider. On 18 April 1775 he made the famous ride to Lexington to warn the patriot leaders, Samuel Adams and John Hancock, that a British force was coming to arrest them and seize the munitions stored at Concord. Revere was immortalised by Henry Longfellow in his celebrated poem of 1861, Paul Revere's Ride. After the war he prospered as a silversmith and iron-founder.

ROCHAMBEAU 1725-1807 Commander of the French forces in America for 1780. His 5,000 troops were crucially important in the siege of Yorktown and Cornwallis arranged for his sword to be surrendered to Rochambeau and not to Washington as a gesture that the French, not the Americans, had defeated the British. Rochambeau then lent £10,000 to Cornwallis.

SHELBURNE, Lord, 1737-1808 A Whig friend of America. As prime minister briefly in 1782–83 agreed the peace terms with America, but won few people's trust as he was too clever by half.

TARLETON, Sir Banastre, 1754-1833 Having gambled away his family fortune, which came from the slave trade, he went to America as a soldier in 1775. Renowned for his courage, impetuosity and utter ruthlessness in the cavalry warfare in the South. A hate figure in America, a hero in Britain, he liked his nickname – 'Bloody Ban'.

WASHINGTON, George, 1732-1799 A poor general but a brilliant leader. Without him the politicians would never have won independence. The army he fashioned sustained the revolution. As First President of the United States of America, 1787-1795, he was in effect King George. He deserved his heroic status.

Picture Credits

With special thanks to Andrew Edmunds; Sara Willett Duke, Curator, Popular & Applied Graphic Art, Prints & Photographs Division, Library of Congress; and Roberta Waddell, Curator of Prints, New York Public Library.

American Antiquarian Society
Atwater Kent Museum
Bloomsbury Auctions
Boston Athenaeum
Boston Fine Art
Bridgeman Art
Trustees of the British Museum
Anne S K Brown Military Collection
Brown University Library, Military Collection
John Carter Brown Library at Brown University
The Colonial Williamsburg Foundation
Connecticut Historical Society
Emmet Collection, Miriam and Ira D Wallach, New York Public Library
Historical Society of Pennsylvania
Library of Congress
National Army Museum
New York Historical Society
New York Public Library
Library Company of Philadelphia